Federalism and Internal Conflicts

Series Editors

Soeren Keil
Canterbury Christ Church University
Canterbury, UK

Eva Maria Belser
University of Freiburg
Freiburg, Switzerland

This series engages in the discussions on federalism as a tool of internal conflict resolution. Building on a growing body of literature on the use of federalism and territorial autonomy to solve ethnic, cultural, linguistic and identity conflicts, both in the West and in non-Western countries, this global series assesses to what extent different forms of federalism and territorial autonomy are being used as tools of conflict resolution and how successful these approaches are.

We welcome proposals on theoretical debates, single case studies and short comparative pieces covering topics such as:

- Federalism and peace-making in contemporary intra-state conflicts
- The link between federalism and democratization in countries facing intra-state conflict
- Secessionism, separatism, self-determination and power-sharing
- Inter-group violence and the potential of federalism to transform conflicts
- Successes and failures of federalism and other forms of territorial autonomy in post-conflict countries
- Federalism, decentralisation and resource conflicts
- Peace treaties, interim constitutions and permanent power sharing arrangements
- The role of international actors in the promotion of federalism (and other forms of territorial autonomy) as tools of internal conflict resolution
- Federalism and state-building
- Federalism, democracy and minority protection

For further information on the series and to submit a proposal for consideration, please get in touch with Ambra Finotello ambra.finotello@palgrave.com, or series editors Soeren Keil soeren.keil@canterbury.ac.uk and Eva Maria Belser evamaria.belser@unifr.ch.

More information about this series at
http://www.palgrave.com/gp/series/15730

Dele Babalola

The Political Economy of Federalism in Nigeria

palgrave
macmillan

Dele Babalola
Department of International Relations
and Diplomacy
Baze University
Abuja, Nigeria

Federalism and Internal Conflicts
ISBN 978-3-030-05492-2 ISBN 978-3-030-05493-9 (eBook)
https://doi.org/10.1007/978-3-030-05493-9

Library of Congress Control Number: 2018963739

This Palgrave Macmillan imprint is published by the registered company Springer Nature Switzerland AG
The registered company address is: Gewerbestrasse 11, 6330 Cham, Switzerland

Preface

Nigeria's federal system is shaped by the country's political economy, which predominantly revolves around oil rents. The central feature of Nigeria's political economy is the convoluted relationship between oil and the state. This book, therefore, brings to the fore the intrinsic link between oil resources and the country's practice of federalism. The federal government oversees the distribution of centrally generated oil revenue. The desire to operate an efficient federal system has often resulted in the adoption of several fiscal principles dictated by a combination of factors, yet the federal system has continuously come under attack from ethno-regional groups. The main argument in this book is that the inability of the federal government to distribute the oil wealth fairly is the main source of the dysfunctional character of the federal system. The colonial legacy of the Federation, the complex ethnic diversity, long years of military rule and ingrained corruption have combined to bring about this verdict. None of these individual factors can be completely ignored in explaining this failure, because they interact in a complicated fashion such that it is difficult to untangle them. The Nigerian federal system is largely flawed and is in serious need of reforms. A political restructuring of the oil-rich federation in ways that would grant the sub-national units some real fiscal autonomy would be a useful reform that might ultimately provide a cure to the ailing federal system.

This book is a revised and enlarged version of my doctoral thesis submitted to the School of Politics and International Relations, University of Kent, Canterbury, United Kingdom. Therefore, my appreciation goes first, to the James Madison Trust for awarding me a scholarship to conduct a doctoral research work. My lead supervisor, late Professor Michael Burgess, whose knowledge of federalism I have immensely benefited from deserves praise. To my second supervisor, Dr. Frank Grundig, I thank him for his invaluable contribution to the thesis. As a teacher and the 'head' of the 'federalist family' at the Centre for Federal Studies, University of Kent, Professor Burgess 'raised' a number of young scholars of federalism. I pay tribute to him for his mentorship. I should also like to pay tribute to my external examiner, late Professor Abdul-Raufu Mustapha who encouraged me to transform the thesis into a book.

I should like to express my profound thanks to Baze University, Abuja, Nigeria for granting me research leave in the summer of 2018 to enable me complete the work. Several other individuals have in varying degrees contributed to the success of the work, among them Dr. Hakeem Onapajo, who read the entire manuscript and made valuable suggestions for improvement and Professor Sadeeque Abba for his critique of some portions of the manuscript. My thanks also go to Professor Member George-Genyi whose critical comments and suggestions on the political economy chapter proved highly valuable. Thanks also go to Professor Kayode Omojuwa and Dr. Chukwuemeka Okafor for their insightful discussions with me on the issue of fiscal federalism in Nigeria. I am also indebted to the late retired Justice Mustapha Akanbi and Dr. Abiodun Adeniyi for sharing with me their thoughts on corruption in Nigeria. Dr. Adeniyi and Dr. Okafor also assisted in editing some portions of the work. My thanks also go to my colleagues in the Department of International Relations and Diplomacy, Baze University, particularly, Professor Osita Agbu whose comments on 'restructuring' I found very helpful. Others are Maryam Datti Ibrahim, Dr. Ebi Seyeifa, Adoyi Omale, Mukhtar Imam, Dr. Ismail Bello, Mercy Kwabe and Zakari Ismail. I also thank Professor Solomon A. Benjamin for his encouragements. However, the views expressed in the book are entirely mine and I take full responsibility for them.

My gratitude also go to Palgrave Macmillan for their professional handling of the publication process, the anonymous reviewers whose comments were useful for style improvements, the Senior Editor, Ambra Finotello and the Series Editors, Dr. Soeren Keil and Dr. E. M. Belser.

Finally, my special thanks go to my amazing wife, Yinka Folaranmi-Babalola, my two sons, Kolapo and Opeyemi, and my little princess, Rennie, without whose support, tolerance, sacrifice and encouragement, this work would not have been completed.

Abuja, Nigeria
October 2018

Dele Babalola

Contents

Abbreviations

AG	Action Group
APC	All Progressives Congress
CDC	Constitution Drafting Committee
CGAR	Crisis Group Africa Report
CPI	Corruption Perceptions Index
DPA	Distributable Pool Account
EPRDF	Ethiopian Peoples' Revolutionary Democratic Front
EU	European Union
FCT	Federal Capital Territory
FGN	Federal Government of Nigeria
FMG	Federal Military Government
GDP	Gross Domestic Product
GNP	Gross National Product
ICGR	International Crisis Group Report
IPOB	Indigenous People of Biafra
IYC	Ijaw Youth Council
LGA	Local Government Area
MASSOB	Movement for the Actualisation of the Sovereign State of Biafra
MEND	Movement for the Emancipation of the Niger Delta
MOSOP	Movement for the Survival of the Ogoni People
NATO	North Atlantic Treaty Organisation
NCNC	National Council of Nigerian Citizens
NDA	Niger Delta Avengers
NDBDA	Niger Delta Basin Development Authority
NDDB	Niger Delta Development Board
NDDC	Niger Delta Development Commission

NDMF	Niger Delta Minorities Forum
NDPVF	Niger Delta People's Volunteer Force
NPC	Northern People's Congress
NPN	National Party of Nigeria
NRMAFC	National Revenue Mobilisation, Allocation and Fiscal Commission
NSWF	National Sovereign Wealth Fund
OMPADEC	Oil Minerals Producing Areas Development Commission
OPC	O'odua People's Congress
OPEC	Organisation of the Petroleum Exporting Countries
OSCE	Organisation for Security and Cooperation in Europe
RCMP	Royal Canadian Mounted Police
RNC	Royal Niger Company
SDP	Social Democratic Party
SGA	Special Grants Account
SJA	Special Joint Account
SPDC	Shell Petroleum Development Company
UAC	United Africa Company
UNDP	United Nations Development Programme

List of Figures and Tables

CHAPTER 1

Introduction: Conceptual Approaches to Nigerian Federalism

Introduction

Federalism as a governmental system became popular as a means of nation-building at the end of the Second World War, especially in the British Commonwealth. The British imperial powers promoted the federal idea in many of its ex-colonies, including Canada, India and Nigeria, perhaps as the most viable option for a multi-cultural country. Likewise, in the post-Cold War era, there was an increased interest in the federal system, as it was increasingly conceived as a tool of conflict management in war-torn countries based on experiences in Bosnia and Herzegovina (BiH) (1995), Ethiopia (1995), and Iraq (2003). Given its utility in multi-dimensional ways, federalism is adopted for different reasons by different countries, in response to disparate situations. The system is particularly attractive to such countries with large size and population as Australia, India, Nigeria and the United States of America. It is also appealing to countries with a high degree of social heterogeneity as Ethiopia, India and Nigeria as a means to achieving unity.

In the 1950s, for example, there was high optimism for federalism in Africa due to the suitability of the system to the heterogeneity that exists in those societies (Burgess 2012a). This optimism, however, disappeared with the collapse of federations like Rhodesia and Nyasaland (1953–1963) and many more. In India and Nigeria, for example, besides the British federal instinct (see, for instance, Burgess 2007) and the desire of

D. Babalola, *The Political Economy of Federalism in Nigeria*, Federalism and Internal Conflicts,
https://doi.org/10.1007/978-3-030-05493-9_1

the individual founding fathers, the recognition of diversity constitutes the driving force behind the formation of the federations. In these two countries, the federal system was adopted to 'hold together' the diverse elements inhabiting the countries (Stepan 1999).

Nigeria, being a product of colonialism, was a victim of a problematic unification of two protectorates, which saw peoples of diverse linguistic, historical, religious and cultural backgrounds brought together. The plural nature of the state made a unitary form of government seemingly unrealistic, making the adoption of federalism in 1954 a pragmatic decision. Therefore, the most significant step taken by Nigerian leaders, with the active support of the British colonial government in response to the country's ethnic diversity was the adoption of a federal political framework. Unlike the American federation, where small units desired to 'come together' and cede to the federal government some measure of their sovereignty, the Nigerian federation was born from a hitherto unitary state (Stepan 1999).

The British had promoted the federal idea in Nigeria hoping that the regions with their different economic resources would complement each other. Moreover, they had hoped that their architectural design would produce a structure capable of reconciling the different diversities in the country, or simply put, that the design would produce unity in a country of over 350 ethnic groups.[1] Likewise, the country's founding fathers had hoped that the interests of the multifarious groups would be better protected under a federal political arrangement. Thus, federalism was both promoted and championed as an instrument of unity in diversity. Contrary to the optimism expressed by the architects of the idea (including the British colonial government), the country's diversity appeared to be an encumbrance on the system. We are not in any way suggesting that diversity in itself is the problem, rather the manner in which the elites have continuously manipulated ethnic and religious sentiments, among others, has become a source of the problem. A federal idea seems appropriate to the socio-political situation of Nigeria but the structural imbalance inherent in the society has made the framework less able to cope with the hydra-headed strains that result from a federal system. Problems of bringing together different peoples continue to provoke debate and

[1] Nigeria is one of the most ethnically diverse countries in the world with approximately 185 million people. The actual number of ethnic groups in Nigeria is not known but some scholars have identified between 350 and 400.

controversy. Accusations of inequalities in the federal structure continue to dominate political discourse.

The Nigerian federation inherited from the colonial government a three-region federal system but its leaders have since increased the number of constituent units to its current thirty-six.[2] At inception, the federation had four notable features. One was the entrenchment of a tripartite system of government with each component unit consisting of a dominant ethnic group and a host of minority groups. Each of the units—the Northern, Western and Eastern Region—was large enough to form a country of its own. Riker (1964, p. 31) confirmed this, noting that Nigeria was the 'only one of ex-British federalisms that does not display the unification of a number of separate colonies no one of which would have been viable alone'. This 'arrangement', coupled with the regionalisation of the national economy, afforded regional bourgeoisie the opportunity to compete amongst themselves for regional political power (Williams 1976, pp. 25–28), which was regarded as a prerequisite for economic power, which in turn was a prerequisite for power acquisition at the federal level. The result was the ruthless ethno-regional competitions, which continue to characterise politics in the country. At a point, the struggle took the form of two regions conspiring against the third, as was demonstrated during the Western Region crisis of 1962 and in the creation of the Mid-Western Region in 1963. Furthermore, politics during this period revolved around a system of patronage, in which regional governments were turned into conduits for private capital accumulation. The ruthless struggle for state patronage culminated in the collapse of the country's first attempt at a federal system, which saw the emergence of the military on the political stage in 1966.

Another feature was that the federal structure was a reflection of the cultural, political and economic differences among the three largest ethnic groups in the country—the Hausa-Fulani, Yoruba, and Igbo—which dominated the Northern, Western and Eastern Regions respectively. In fact, the system was equated with regionalism because the units were in line with the ethnic structure of the country (Awa 1976, p. 2).

[2] In Nigeria, between 1954 when the country became a federation and 1966 when the military seized power, constituent units were referred to as 'Regions' but these came to be known as 'States' after 1966. Therefore, in this study, 'State' is used to connote constituent/sub-national/sub-federal/federating/component unit and these terms are used interchangeably.

To use Kirk-Greene's (1967, p. 5) word, these regions were not as 'self-contained' as they looked, as each consisted of the majority and other minority ethnic groups, and the majority dominated the minorities. In the Northern Region, for instance, are other ethnic groups such as the Kanuri, the Tiv, the Igala, the Igbira and so on, which when put together, constitute a large chunk of the country's population. The Region was not an ethnic entity, and the same was true of the Eastern Region where one finds the Ibibio, Efik and other peoples, and in the Western Region where we find such minority groups as the Benin and Edo to mention a few.

This tripartite 'design' seemingly put the fate of the country in the hands of the three major ethnic groups, setting the stage for a triangular struggle for the country's resources. The arrangement also resulted in the majority/minority dichotomy, as well as the marginalisation of the minority groups that continue to shape the politics of the country. The implication of this tripodal structure for the minority groups is best captured by Nnoli (1995) who observed that the minorities were only important as resources for the majority groups to strengthen the latter's political power or to weaken the power of their rivals in other Regions. This development set the tone for the politics of the country. Therefore, one main challenge that confronted Nigerian leaders following decolonisation was how to genuinely bring together the different peoples brought together by British imperialism. Nigerian leaders have had to contend with the daunting task of ensuring that Nigerians continue to live together in harmony and within a single political unit as envisaged by the British.

Yet another feature was that the Northern Region was bigger than the other two Regions combined, thereby affording it the opportunity to out-compete both the Western and Eastern Regions. This period marked the beginning of the fear of political and economic domination usually expressed by regional elites; a fear heightened by the economic disparities in the Regions. A federal arrangement in which one constituent unit is excessively big negates the principle of equality of states (Macmahon 1962, p. 7; Wheare 1963, p. 50).

A further feature was that the federating units, due to their enormous resources, enjoyed substantial political and economic powers. Nolte (2002) refers to the federal system, as constituted then, as regional federalism because the federal arrangement was such that the component units were constitutionally allowed to enjoy extensive political and financial autonomy. The units were so powerful that the centre was subordinated to the Regions to the extent that, in the event of a conflict, for example, regional laws took precedence over federal laws in the areas of joint legislative competence (Ayoade 1988, p. 23).

These features, however, disappeared with the emergence of the military on the political stage, an era coinciding with that of the oil boom. The increased inflow of oil rents into Nigeria's economy in the early 1970s gave way to a new era of politically and economically strong federal centre. This completed the transformation of the country from a peripheralised to a highly centralised federation. This transformation brings to the fore the link between Nigeria's oil and the practice of federalism. What Suberu (2001) refers to as the 'hyper-centralisation' of resources is fundamentally at the heart of the imperfection characterising the operation of federalism in the oil-rich federation. Over-centralisation has become the defining feature of Nigeria's federal system. If federalism is typically a non-centralised system, then all is not well with Nigeria's federal system. The increasing agitation for 'true federalism', especially in the current democratic dispensation is an indication that the system is defective.

The Nigerian state has since the oil boom of 1973 operated an oil-centred economy. Prior to the emergence of oil as the principal source of foreign exchange earnings, Nigeria's economic success revolved around agriculture. The economic centrality of the federal centre, resulting also from the necessities of the civil war (1967–1970), ensured a complete concentration of resources at the centre. As resources become increasingly concentrated at the centre, so, the constituent units became politically and economically impotent. Moreover, the centre became a battleground for ethno-regional competition for federal economic resources and political power. In all of these, the federal government remains domineering, overseeing the distribution of oil rents. The source of centralisation goes back to 1966 when the military first intervened in Nigerian politics through coup d'état. The military did not just intervene, they actually entrenched a system characterised by 'tightly centralised controls' (Suberu 2001, pp. 1–2). Given its command structure, a military rule may be likened to a unitary system of government. Clearly, the military's style of administration seriously affected the operation of federalism in Nigeria.

In an ideal federal arrangement, governments at all levels are expected to have an independent revenue base, but this is not the case in Nigeria where the present thirty-six states and the Federal Capital Territory (FCT) depend heavily on the centre for sustenance. This is a negation of the federal principle, which enjoins every constituent unit to be self-financing. Wheare (1963, p. 51) particularly emphasised the significance of the economic viability of the constituent units to the formation, operation and survival of a federation. He argued that the units must possess sufficient economic resources to support themselves as well as the central government. Thus, a weak independent revenue base among Nigeria's constituent units makes the sharing of centrally-collected revenue a norm. The sharing is, however, loaded with contentions. One reason for the usual acrimony is that the constituent units lack viable sources of revenue of their own, and by implication, find it extremely difficult to discharge their constitutional duties without fiscal transfers from the centre. Another source of contention has been a lack of consensus among the contending parties on a revenue-sharing formula, as every constituent unit, as well as every ethnic group, wants to maximise its share of the national resources (Elaigwu 2007, p. 204). The political sensitivity of revenue sharing has also been compounded by the 'perceptions of regional ethnic dominance' among the ethnic minorities (Baker 1984, p. v).

By the time a democratic rule was re-established in 1999, after thirteen years of military dictatorship, the character of Nigerian federalism had significantly changed from 'bottom-heavy' as it was at inception, to 'top-heavy' with political and economic power concentrated at the centre. As expected in a deeply divided society, the centralisation of oil revenue increased the ruthless competition for state control by ethno-regional elites who always find it convenient to politicise ethnicity and other social cleavages in their quest for economic advancement. This explains why the operation of federalism in the current democratic dispensation has been significantly dominated by the quest for an equitable revenue sharing practice.

The re-establishment of a liberal democratic rule in 1999 kick-started a resurgence of ethnic and regional agitations manifesting mainly in the clamour for 'true federalism'. At the forefront of this campaign were the Yoruba elite of the south-west who had not hidden their ill-feeling for their Hausa-Fulani counterparts for the annulment of the 1993 presidential election, believed to have been won by a Yoruba man. Fear of marginalisation, real and imagined, by the country's ethnic minority groups, which dates back to the 1950s, when out of fear of domination, clamoured for separate constituent units, also deepened in the post-1999 period, particularly in the Niger Delta region, where the bulk of oil is derived. There is the perception in the area that the majority ethnic groups, because of their control of political power at the centre, are reaping from the national wealth more than their contribution. Regional elite decries the perceived lopsided nature of Nigerian distributive politics, which in their belief, is inimical to their local interests. They argue that the oil found in their region should be a source of economic fortunes for the region and its people and not a source of despondency. Also, having complained of marginalisation, some Igbo elites in the south-east region threatened to pull the region away from the federation. Another major development immediately following the return of civilian rule was the Sharia issue, which developed into a sectarian violence.[3] The adoption of the Sharia by twelve states in the north in 1999 was perceived in some quarters to be an outcome of feelings of marginalisation harboured by the Northern elite in the new political dispensation (Abah 2006). At the heart of these seemingly different agitations was the distribution of the country's oil-generated wealth.

In an attempt to ensure a fair distribution of political and economic resources, the political elites have developed some distributive and structural frameworks, some of which are in line with those suggested by Donald Horowitz, but all of which have failed to achieve the desired outcome. According to Horowitz (2000, p. 596), distributive policies are aimed at changing 'the ethnic balance of economic opportunities and rewards', while the structural approach aims to change 'the political framework in which ethnic conflict occurs'. The adoption of different resource-allocation formulas and the 'federal character' principle are examples of the federation's distributive policies. The federal character principle aims to provide representation for all major ethnic groups in cabinet positions and in the civil service, while formulas for the distribution of oil revenue are aimed at ensuring equitable distribution. The main structural approach the political elites have embarked upon includes the division of the country into smaller components through state creation. It was thought that dividing the country into several

[3] Sharia is a body of Islamic religious law regulating all aspects of Muslim life. It is based on the Quran, the Islamic holy book, and the Hadith, a narration of Mohammed's (the Prophet of Islam) life, and his teachings.

constituent units would reduce the fierce competition for patronage to the constituent unit level (see, for example, Dent 2000).

Central to the issue of wealth distribution in Nigeria has been the continual debate over the application of the principle of derivation. Derivation is the method of distributing centrally generated revenues to the constituent units of the federation in relation to the contribution made by each to the country's larger revenue. In an attempt to ensure a fair distribution of national wealth, the Nigerian state has adopted several fiscal principles but derivation has particularly generated the most controversy. This is because each ethno-regional group wants maximum benefits from the country's commonwealth. The current debate, for instance, revolves around what proportion of the country's oil-generated revenues should go to the oil-producing states. There is little doubt that the inability of Nigeria's federal system to ensure an equitable distribution of resources is compounded by the over-centralisation that characterises the system.

Following the foregoing analyses, it is convenient to argue that the character of Nigeria's federal system is shaped by the country's political economy, which entrenches oil-dependency. There is a dialectical relationship between the domestic political economy and the federal system, and the former shapes the latter. The aim of the study, therefore, is to demonstrate that the economic centrality of the federal government, manifesting in the distribution of the country's resources is at the heart of the country's dysfunctional federal system. It is also important to investigate if the federal system corresponds to or conflicts with the principles of federalism and the practices of established federations. In doing this, we try to explore the meaning, as well as the essential characteristics of federalism. Moreover, we also examine the traditional approaches to the study of federalism. In what follows, therefore, the conceptualisation of federalism, federation, and confederation is expounded.

Federalism, Federation and Confederation: Conceptual Clarification

Defining certain terms, which are considered relevant to the study of federalism, is also important. It is now becoming increasingly customary in federal studies to define such terms as federalism, federation, and confederation, and treat them as separate concepts in order to avoid their misuse. Conceptual clarification between federalism, federation, and confederation is particularly important because the terms mean different things. The difference between federation and confederation also has some implications for the practice of federalism in Nigeria, especially in the light of the growing clamour for the return to genuine federalism or what has been referred to as 'true federalism' in Nigerian parlance. As we shall see later, some political leaders, commentators and activists, in their campaign for a more functional federal system, show some misconception of federalism.

There seems to be a consensus among the Anglo-American writers on federalism that Preston King was the first to observe the distinction, particularly between 'federalism' and 'federation' in his book, *Federalism and Federation* first published in 1982. In that study, he lamented that most writers 'make no distinction at all' between these terms (p. 20). It must, however, be mentioned that the eminent Nigerian professor of Political Science, Eme Awa had, in his book *Issues in Federalism*, published in 1976 drawn our attention to the interchangeable use of the terms 'federal, confederal and federation, confederation and confederacy' by the American founding fathers as if the terms mean the same thing (p. 1). He argued that in its modern usage, a confederation is different from a federation in that a confederation is 'a union of states which retain their independent status…' (p. 1) whereas, in a federation 'neither the central nor the regional governments are subordinate to each other' (p. 4). Following on from King, Burgess (1993, p. 12) also observed that most political analysts often allude to 'federalism when they really mean federation', and 'some scholars still use the terms "federalism" and "federation" interchangeably to refer to both a process and a terminal end-point'. Likewise, Verney (1995, p. 82) noted that 'federalism' is often treated as synonymous with 'federation'. It is clear from the foregoing observations that there is a degree of unanimity that federalism, federation and confederation mean different things and should be treated differently. So, let us start with the definition of federalism.

Federalism, like many social science concepts such as justice, and freedom, for example, is an ambiguous concept and difficult to define. In fact, Birch (1966, p. 15) and Duchacek (1970, p. 189) described federalism as a concept with no fixed meaning. Federalism means different things to different people. The difficulty in defining this concept has not stopped earlier writers from bequeathing on us some valuable definitions.

To this end, therefore, federalism has been defined variously as a principle (Wheare 1963), a political philosophy and an ideological position that promotes regional independence and autonomy (King 1982, p. 74); a 'political principle' involving 'the constitutional diffusion of power' between the central and the constituent governments to achieve self-rule and shared rule (Elazar 1987, pp. 5–6; see also, Elazar 1973, p. 3); and as a 'value concept' that informs federation (Burgess 2006, p. 2).

Federalism may mean different things to different people but what seems to be constant about this system of government is the intrinsic 'principle' that distinguishes the system from others. This principle, which Wheare had called the *federal principle* makes federalism very unique and has been defined as the 'method of dividing powers so that the general and regional governments are each, within a sphere, co-ordinate and independent' (Wheare 1963, p. 10). Key to this definition is the issue of division of powers and the idea that each tier of government should be independent of each other. Interrogating the notion of independence as used in this definition is very important as this is what distinguishes a federation from a confederation, which is also an association of states but in which 'the general government is dependent upon the regional governments' (Wheare 1963, p. 32). By 'independent', Wheare meant a system in which each tier of government has its own independent functions and neither has supreme authority over the other. Another interpretation of this definition is that neither the central nor the regional governments are subordinate to each other.

Wheare's postulation, no doubt, poses the problem of application because it is not practicable for the central government and the regional governments not to depend on each other for one thing or another. Some measure of interdependence and cooperation in areas that touch on the lives of the citizens are crucial to the successful operation of any given federal system. The success of the American federal system, for example, is built on the interdependence between the federal and state governments. If the federal government is to be efficient, the federal principle must allow for some degree of flexibility. These problems aside, the notion of federal principle has been described as Wheare's most important conceptual legacy to the study of federalism (Burgess 2012b, p. 38). This legacy has continued to shape our understanding of federalism. Wheare's definition of federalism, as well as his notion of the federal principle, became the most widely accepted, especially when the question of comparing federal systems of government arises. His classic study entitled, *Federal Government*, first published in 1946 is the first work on federalism to provide the student of political science with an inroad into the study of federalism.

Federalism may be suffering from conceptual ambiguity; what is, nonetheless, clear is that it emphasises the division of powers between, at least, two tiers of government. This is what distinguishes a federal political system from a unitary system. Therefore, by federalism, we mean a system of government in which powers are shared between the central government and the constituent units, and as a political system, it promotes the autonomy of the federating governments within the federation. Federalism is simply about shared sovereignty. Having defined federalism, let us attempt to define federation.

The term federation has been taken to mean a political institution, a state or group of states. K. C. Wheare, who modelled his notion of federalism along the lines of the American model, defined federation as:

> an association of states so organised that powers are divided between a general government, which in certain matters – for example, the making of treaties and the coining of money – is independent of the government of the associated states, and, on the other hand, state governments which in certain matters are, in their turn, independent of the general government. (Wheare 1963, p. 2)

Implicit in Wheare's definition is that in a federation, two or more tiers of government exist and both share governmental powers. In addition, each has its separate powers. Moreover, each draws authority from the citizens whom they are, in turn, answerable to.

While agreeing with Wheare's definition, Riker (1964, p. 5) added that in a federation, both the general government and the constituent governments rule over the same territory and people and each government is constitutionally empowered to make some decisions independently of the other. Similarly, Ivo Duchacek in his book *Comparative Federalism: The Territorial Dimension of Politics*, first published in 1970, also perceived federation as a polity in which political authority is territorially divided between two autonomous governments—the general and the constituent governments. For King (1982, p. 77), federation means an institutional arrangement, taking the form of a sovereign state, and distinguished from other such states solely by the fact that its central government incorporates regional units into its decision procedure on some constitutionally entrenched basis. Burgess (1993, p. 5; 2006, p. 2) takes federation to mean an empirical reality with structures and institutions, or simply a sovereign state.

The foregoing definitions are strikingly similar. Central to them, however, is that in a federation, there exist, at least, two independent tiers of government whose existence is entrenched in a written constitution. There is also a division of powers between the constitutionally recognised units. Moreover, neither tier is subordinate to the other. Finally, the levels of government are directly elected and each act directly upon the citizens. As mentioned earlier, these are the important pillars of a federation. Thus, by federation, we mean a sovereign state in which there is a territorial division of power between the central/general/federal government and the constituent/federating/state governments. The central government has authority over the whole territory while the constituent governments exercise authority over their respective territories. In many federations, including Nigeria, the federal government possesses exclusive power over such matters as defence, currency, foreign affairs, to mention a few. Another critical feature of a federation, as noted by scholars, is the presence of a federal government, which is an independent authority for the whole country in respect of some matters.

These attributes, individually or collectively, are supposed to bring about good government. Although, as Wheare (1963, p. 34) cautioned, 'federal government is not always and everywhere good government' but a means to good government. So, besides the reason of good government, what are the other objectives of federations? The overall objective of all federations, including Nigeria, as argued by Elazar (1987, p. 12), is to express 'self-rule plus shared rule' through the distribution of powers between those assigned to the federal government for common purposes and those assigned to the constituent units for purposes of local autonomy and the preservation of specific identities and interests. This assertion, no doubt derives from Elazar's view that a federation is an outcome of a covenant between the general government and the regional governments.

At the risk of committing a tautology, we state at this stage that the concept of federalism is different from that of federation, and should not be used interchangeably. While the former means a governmental system that allows independent and shared rule, the latter connotes a form of sovereign state designed by political architects to achieve unity, while also preserving the diversity of the country. However, taking federation to mean a state may be oversimplifying the concept. Federation may not necessarily be a state but a union of 'separate political communities' united by one or more common objectives, but retaining their distinctive group character for other purposes (Friedrich 1968, p. 7). This definition implies that a federation may be an alliance of sovereign states such as the European Union or the African Union. In these two unions, independent states have come together for some common political, but mostly economic objectives. In this study, however, by federation, we mean a sovereign state like Australia, Canada, India, Nigeria and the United States.

Having cast some light on the conceptual differences between federalism and federation, we should now proceed to examine the meaning of confederation or confederacy, a notion usually contrasted with that of federation. A confederation differs from a federation in the sense that a confederation is a union of states, which is less binding in its character when compared with a federation. The states in a confederation retain their independent status, as well as enjoy a high degree of autonomy. More importantly, the units in a confederacy are sovereign and independent while the general (confederal) authority is relatively weak. The unique feature of this system is that a confederal authority is dependent upon the states that have come together to form the union (Wheare 1963, p. 32). In a confederacy, substantial governmental powers remain with the original states, which also retain their separate identities. This is not suggesting that certain specified powers are not surrendered to the central government for common purposes such as mutual security but this is usually negligible. Another significant feature of a confederation is that the confederal government does not exercise authority over the citizens who relate directly to their own separate component governments and indirectly to the confederal government. The opposite is the case in a federation where there is a direct relationship between citizens and their states, as well as with the federal government. Examples of confederations include the Swiss Confederation before 1848 and the United States before 1787. The confederal system is no longer fashionable and has been replaced with the federal system. The Americans, for example, jettisoned the confederal system for a relatively perfect union perhaps due to the inherent weaknesses in the system. This is reflected in the Preamble to the United States Constitution which states:

> We the people of the United States, in order to form a more perfect Union, establish Justice, insure domestic tranquillity, provide for the common defence, promote the general welfare, and secure the blessings of liberty to ourselves and our posterity, do ordain and establish this Constitution for the United States of America.

As noted earlier, federation is not an end in itself, but a means to achieve some economic objectives, national unity, as well as good government. But why have these objectives become a mirage in Nigeria? The answer to this question lies in the operation of the governmental system. As we shall see shortly, Nigeria's federal system is deficient in character. Scholars of federalism have identified a series of features vital to federalism. Macmahon (1962, pp. 4–5) described these characteristics as 'essential attributes' while Jinadu (2016, pp. 28–29) has described them as the 'pillars' of federations (see also Livingston 1956, pp. 9–11; Wheare 1963, pp. 10–14). These fundamental features are outlined as follows.

One, a federation comprises of one general/central and several constituent governments which are coordinate with one another, and each is independent of each other within its sphere. Depending on the constitutional design, some constituent units design their forms of government as they desire. Of course, Nigeria consists of a general government, 36 state and 774 local governments but, in practice, the state governments are not autonomous of the federal government. Two, federalism presupposes also the constitutional division of powers between the general and constituent governments in such a manner that those assigned to the constituent units 'must be substantial and not merely trivial' (Macmahon 1962, p. 4). Federalism is not just about the division of powers; it is also about ensuring that powers are not excessively concentrated in either the federal or the constituent governments. In other words, federalism should be non-centralised. Nigeria's federal system is over-centralised both in theory and practice. Three, the general government relates directly with the citizens, both 'to draw authority from them' through periodic elections and 'for the purpose of exacting taxes' (Macmahon 1962, p. 4). In Nigeria and other federations, each citizen is subject to both the federal government and the state governments. Four, the existence of a written constitution, which must be supreme and stipulate the responsibilities of each tier of government must be guaranteed if the system is to function effectively. Written constitutions are typically consonant with federal systems. A federal constitution accommodates the conflicting interests within the federal union. Since becoming a federation, Nigeria has had several written constitutions, which have been consistent in spelling out matters on exclusive, concurrent and residual legislative lists. Five, the existence of a bicameral legislature in which the constituent units have equal representation in the Upper House of the central legislature is also essential. Bicameralism facilitates the representation of the interests of citizens in the constituent units at the national level as the second chamber provides for a second opinion (Wheare 1968, p. 140). Except for the periods of military rule (1966–1979 and 1984–1999), Nigeria has been consistent with bicameralism. As presently constituted, the National Assembly, as the country's central legislature is usually known comprises the House of Representatives (Lower House) consisting of 360 members, and the Senate (Upper House) with 109 Senators. As in other federations, Nigeria's Upper House guarantees equal representation of the states irrespective of size, while the Lower House ensures proportional representation. Six, equality of the constituent units in regards to size and population is also imperative. As mentioned above, except in the First Republic (1960–66), constituents units in Nigeria are treated as equal. Seven, also important is the existence of an independent judiciary (Birch 1955, p. 1). A typical modern government comprises three arms or organs of government: the legislature, whose main function is to make laws; the executive, that implements the laws; and the judiciary which interprets the laws. In Nigeria, just like in other federations, the judiciary, not only interprets the constitution, it also adjudicates between the federal and constituent governments.

It is clear from the above that Nigeria's current federal system possesses many of the features of federalism, yet, it is not working the way it should. The key explanation for this is that the system lacks the non-centralised feature. This is the foremost anomaly characterising the system.

Approaches to the Study of Federalism

Federalism, just like any other subject of inquiry, has to be studied within a theoretical context. Indeed, according to Burgess (1993, p. 8), 'federalism must be viewed through conceptual lenses which are sensitised to different political cultures…' Employing an approach to analyse the operation of a given federal system provides an insight into the workings of that system. Using the approach to analyse Nigeria's structures and processes is a distinctly different way of understanding its practice of federalism. Nevertheless, if a solid theoretical foundation is to be laid for the study, then other possible approaches have to be examined. This helps to appreciate their utility to the general study of federalism as well as that of Nigeria. Moreover, it also helps to justify the choice of the political economy approach.

If we accept that federalism has no standard meaning, logically, therefore, the concept does not have a standard theory or an 'accepted theory' (Duchacek 1970, p. 189). Burgess (2006, p. 3) also submitted that 'there is as yet no fully-fledged theory of federalism'. However, several approaches have been developed to analyse the character, as well as the workings of a given federal state. The most commonly competing approaches include the institutional or constitutional approach; sociological approach; political approach; and process or developmental approach. We provide a synopsis of these approaches below.

Institutional or Constitutional Approach

The constitutional approach focuses on the legal framework of a state, that is, its structure and authorities, and the way in which these authorities are distributed among the tiers of government in the federation. K. C. Wheare, the chief proponent of this approach emphasised the role of federal constitutions in institutional design, as well as the legal relations, that is, the constitutional division of powers between the general and the constituent governments. As noted earlier, Wheare had defined federalism in terms of constitutional law and the entrenchment of the division of powers in the constitution.

Scholars after him have, however, argued that his notion of federalism is 'highly legalistic', neglecting some political realities and sociological variables crucial to the working of any federal government (see Riker 1964). Birch (1966, p. 16) has particularly argued that Wheare's approach cannot usefully be applied as a framework of analysis in many of the new federations, including Nigeria, because some of these states do not conform to even Wheare's model of federalism when critically examined. Also, for Dikshit (1975, p. 12), since federalism is concerned with many problems other than legal ones, then 'a purely legal approach to federalism has not sufficed'. Wheare's approach may also be criticised for not paying enough attention to the economic variables in the society.

Wheare possibly saw this barrage of criticism coming when he cautioned that the exclusive examination of a constitution may not be enough to analyse the dynamics of federalism of any given federation.

Perhaps in defence of Wheare, Watts (1966, p. 14) observed that the former was writing at a time when political studies were more a study of legal and constitutional relations. That is, when scholars of federalism concentrated mainly on the legal framework within which the general and regional governments operated. Nonetheless, Watts was still of the view that the legal study of constitutions is not sufficient to explain how federal systems operate because 'excessive legalism' or 'inordinate legalism' tells only one side of the story. In a similar fashion, Macmahon (1972, p. 3), insisted that a federal arrangement is 'legal in essence', and 'the practice is largely administrative'.

It is imperative to state that these criticisms are not enough to render the approach inconsequential. The approach has contributed in no small measure both to the theoretical and empirical understanding of federalism in the sense that, it underscores that a federation requires a written constitution that spells out the operation of a federal political system.

Sociological Approach

The main advocate of the sociological approach was William S. Livingston, who was probably the first to define federalism in sociological terms.[4] In a critique of Wheare's constitutional approach, Livingston posited that federalism is not a function of constitutions but of societies and:

> The essential nature of federalism is to be sought for, not in the shadings of legal and constitutional terminology, but in the forces - economic, social, political, cultural - that have made the outward forms of federalism necessary...The essence of federalism lies not in the institutional or constitutional structure but in the society itself. (Livingston 1952, pp. 83–84; 1956, pp. 1–2)

[4]Livingston's idea on the sociological bases of federalism was first articulated in his seminal article, 'A Note on the Nature of Federalism', *Political Science Quarterly*, Vol. 67, No. LXVII (1952), which was later revised and transformed to a book entitled *Federalism and Constitutional Change*, published in 1956.

As articulated in the above definition, the essence of federalism does not lie in the legal division of powers, but in the societal diversity, that is, the social cleavages inherent in the society, as well as the political salience of these cleavages. For Livingston, a federation is a polity predicated upon regionally grouped diversities and the accommodation of these diversities. It is clear, therefore, that Livingston puts society before the state thereby bringing the subject of federalism in tandem with the political sociology tradition. Political sociology is about how the society affects the state. The key point here is that the interplay between the societal diversity and federalism must not be ignored while studying a particular federal system.

The idea of federalism as a sociological phenomenon also came under criticism. For instance, Birch (1966, pp. 16–18) argued that Livingston failed to develop a suitable alternative approach to the study of federalism because his analysis has the same kind of institutional basis as Wheare's. Another critic of this approach was Watts (1966, p. 15) who argued that the study of federalism is an interplay of the social foundations, the written constitutions and the practices of governments. Yet another critic of the sociological approach was Sawer (1969) who described the idea of conceiving federalism from a sociological perspective as misleading. For Sawer, federalism is a constitutional political system distinct from sociological attitudes for the reason that the choices and compromises involved in its operation require the work of political leaders and legal experts (p. 137). The approach may also be criticised on the ground that, although federalism may ensure adequate representation of the diverse groups that make up the federation, the survival of any political system transcends the issue of representation alone. These criticisms aside, the sociological approach may become useful in studying such a federation as Ethiopia, India and Nigeria where the issue of diversity is fundamental to the adoption of a federal system of government. This key issue is also important to the operation of the governmental system.

Political Approach

One notable critic of the constitutional and sociological approaches was William H. Riker, who used his work *Federalism: Origin, Operation and Significance* originally published in 1964 to suggest that federalism should be analysed via a political lens. For Riker, the maintenance or survival of a federation does not depend on the division of governmental powers as earlier suggested by Wheare because federalism is 'a bargain between prospective national leaders and officials of constituent governments' for certain purposes (Riker 1964, p. 11). Riker's political bargain thesis is explored further in the next chapter. Thus the federal bargain, which ensures that both sides in the bargain for a union enjoy some benefits from the union, drives the formation as well as the operation of a given federation. One major criticism against Riker's political approach is its limitation to study federations like India and Nigeria, for example, where many forces combined to give birth to the federation. Also, the approach does not pay attention to the socioeconomic forces that combined to result in federations or those that shape federal structures. The approach focuses excessively on the political aspects of federalism and using it may not tell the full story of a federation.

Process or Developmental Approach

This approach may be linked to the work of Carl J. Friedrich (1968), who defined federalism as a process rather than a static pattern of government. For Friedrich, federalism is a *process* aimed at achieving a union of divergent groups which retain their individual identity. Scholars of federalism who follow this approach focus on those centripetal and centrifugal forces that culminate in the birth of a given federal state with a view to understanding the complex dynamics of the state. The main criticism against this approach is that it focuses largely on the federalising process and does not give sufficient explanation of when the forces identified by Friedrich could result in a federation or how they contribute to the operation of a federation.

Nigerian Federalism: The Political Economy Approach

It may be summed up now that the constitutional approach of Wheare is too legalistic as it mainly emphasises the constitutional division of governmental powers in a federal state, and the sociological approach of Livingston focuses excessively on social diversity. Likewise, the political approach of Riker is too narrow, focusing only on the political conditions necessary for the formation, as well as the maintenance of a federation, while the process approach of Friedrich focuses only on the federalising process. In addition to these shortcomings, one may say also that the major weakness of these traditionally dominant approaches is that they pay little or no attention to the economic dynamics of a federation. Nevertheless, the approaches cannot be dismissed as being completely irrelevant; any one of them or a combination of them may be adopted in the study of any particular federation. In fact, they have provided us with different routes through which questions bordering on federalism can be answered. For example, some scholars have adopted the sociological approach to analyse the dynamics of federalism in Nigeria. What they do is to examine how the multifaceted diversities have impacted on the practice of federalism in the multi-ethnic country. Others adopt the constitutional approach focusing mainly on the formal division of governmental powers, that is, intergovernmental relations as entrenched in the country's constitution. Those who adopt the sociological approach have come to the conclusion that the inability of the country's federal system to regulate social relations is at the heart of the crisis of the system. Similarly, those who use the constitutional approach are of the view that the problem with the Nigerian state is its constitution which they believe has not been able to manage the relations among the governments of the federation.

Given the above limitations and the nature of the forces that induced the Nigerian federation, it is worthwhile to go beyond the traditional approaches in order to analyse the dynamics of its federal system. This study, therefore, considers an alternative analytical framework, which builds on the traditional approaches but pays more attention to the political and economic forces that impact on the federation. It is highly unlikely that the practice of federalism in the oil-rich federation would be understood without cognisance to the country's larger political economy. This is where an all-encompassing analytical framework such as the political economy approach becomes helpful. As we have seen above, federalism is not just about the constitutional division of powers, the character of political institutions or the accommodation of the diversities in the federation, but it is also about the political economy of the federation. Thus, examining the interaction between politics and economics, and the effects of this interaction on the people of Nigeria on the one hand and on the federation itself on the other is expected to aid our understanding of the practice of federalism in Nigeria. So, what is political economy?

In its classical form, political economy was concerned with how the leaders sourced and distributed funds to all the inhabitants of a society. Indeed, one of the founding fathers of classical political economy, Adam Smith, in his *Wealth of Nations*, defined political economy as a subject concerned with the twin objectives of providing firstly, 'a plentiful revenue or subsistence for the people', or to enable them to provide such revenue or subsistence for themselves; and secondly, to supply the state or commonwealth with a revenue sufficient for the public services (Smith 1776, p. 11, quoted in Eatwell et al. 1987, p. 905). Thus, classical political economy was concerned with the growth and development of an economic system, as well as those political and economic factors which aided or obstructed this growth and development, the interaction of these factors and the consequential effect of this process on the myriad of social groups within the system (Aina 1986, p. 2). In its modern usage, political economy is the study of the interaction of politics and economics. It is concerned with how political factors determine economic outcomes and how economic factors determine political outcomes. More often than not, the dynamic nature of a country's political economy explains how the government of that country is operated.

Generally, the political economy approach contributes to the understanding of how the interaction between the political and economic systems of any given society affects the production and distribution of the society's resources. It also helps to explain the effect of this relationship on the people. Moreover, it also examines the state's political processes and structures in relation to the distribution of economic resources in the state, or in Burgess' words, how far 'economic policy impinges upon constitutional affairs and vice versa' (2006, p. 144). Hence, the political economy approach to the understanding of the practice of federalism is predicated upon the relationship between the political and the economic system of a given federation.

As shall be shown later, Nigeria's oil-centric economy combines with the federal structure to produce a highly centralised federal system. This has contributed significantly to the dysfunctional character of federalism in the country. It, therefore, makes meaning to contend that an examination of the operation of federalism in the oil-rich country can best be undertaken against the backdrop of its larger political economy. The branch of political economy approach considered more adequate to do this is the 'rentier' theory. The rentier political economy is concerned with the consequences of oil dependency on an oil-rich state such as Nigeria and Venezuela, for example. The choice of this theory is predicated on the assumption that other political economy approaches would be inadequate to explain the distribution of Nigeria's oil wealth. For example, the liberal political economy places emphasis on free market and minimal state intervention while the Marxist approach focuses on the primacy of the economic system and the antagonistic relationship between the exploiter and the exploited classes. The latter school studies society in terms of the simple base/superstructure model of the capitalist society and also emphasises the inherent contradictions in the society. For Marx, the base or substructure constitutes the economic foundations of a society, while the superstructure is the social, political and legal relations built upon the base. The base and the superstructure continually interact and this interaction largely shapes the society. However, the Marxist perspective is often criticised for its exclusive focus on the antagonistic relations within the social class forces.

It is clear that federalism is a multifaceted subject and it is not out of character to use one or more of the aforementioned approaches to answer key questions that border on the practice of federalism. However, the choice of the political economy approach is considered appropriate. As noted earlier, the political economy of Nigeria is central to the practice of its federal system. In Nigeria, the political and economic systems overlap and consequently affect the lives of the citizens. Therefore, the approach will explain how this interaction affects the Nigerian federal state on the one hand and the citizens on the other. In other words, we are studying the link between 'the political' and 'the economic' and the effects of this link on Nigeria's federal structure and its citizens. But this is not to be done to the complete exclusion of other approaches, especially the sociological approach (ethnicity variable). As Diamond (1988, p. 21) rightly noted, 'Nothing can be understood about Nigeria until its pattern of ethnic diversity is delineated'.

It is now worth reiterating that the fundamental purpose of this study is to utilise the political economy approach to explain why federalism in Nigeria has been a source of controversy rather than a uniting factor. The study also aims to contribute to the understanding of the dynamics of federalism in a multi-ethnic state like Nigeria, and also make an addition to the growing body of literature on the study of federalism. Moreover, the continuing debate among scholars and political commentators about the utility of federalism in Nigeria or the extent to which Nigeria can be considered a successful or failed federal state, especially in the light of rising agitations by ethno-regional groups for 'true federalism', makes the study a worthwhile exercise. It is, in fact, not out of place to describe the study as an attempt to join the debate on the efficacy of federalism in Nigeria.

Structure of the Work

The work is organised into seven chapters including this introductory chapter.

Chapter 2 provides an analysis of the formation of the Nigerian federation focusing on the centripetal and centrifugal forces that coalesced to result in the federation. The origin of the Nigerian federation has elicited two contrasting perspectives. Some scholars have argued that the presence of certain socio-economic conditions induced the federation while others are of the view that the British colonial government purposely imposed federalism on Nigeria in order to maintain a neo-colonial control of the country after their departure. The key argument in this chapter is that to reject the social and economic conditions that laid the foundation for the federation is to render insignificant the importance of the forces that resulted in the transformation of the previously unitary state into a federation. The practice of federalism in Nigeria cannot be fully understood without understanding the character of the society. The chapter, therefore, further highlights the key elements of the country's federal society and how they impact on the practice of federalism in the country.

In Chapter 3, we examine the political economy of Nigeria. Since the study is about how Nigeria's political economy shapes the country's federal system, it is imperative to examine the character of the domestic political economy in detail. In doing so, attention is paid to the salient feature of the political economy, namely, oil dependency. The aim of this chapter is to analyse the centrality of oil to the political economy of the country, and the intrinsic relationship between this natural resource and the Nigerian state.

Chapter 4 provides an understanding of how over-centralisation of the federal system impact on resource distribution in the oil-rich federation. The aim is to establish the extent to which Nigeria's revenue allocation system or fiscal federalism can be said to conform with or deviate from existing theories and practices. In Nigeria, the sharing of centrally-generated revenues is entrenched in the federal constitution, yet revenue allocation has not ceased to be a contentious issue because of the response of the federating units to the character of the economy which breeds an over-centralised federal system. In line with the central argument of the study, this chapter examines the political economy of revenue allocation with the aim of demonstrating how the domestic political economy shapes federalism in Nigeria.

Chapter 5 focuses on how the unequal distribution of Nigeria's wealth has contributed to the fear of marginalisation, which has resulted in conflicts and ultimately, political instability. In this chapter, we discuss the series of the threat of secession and agitations for self-determination, as well as the actual attempt by the then Eastern Region, populated mainly by the Igbo ethnic group to secede. Discussing the civil war also contributes to our understanding of the part the war economy played in the excessive centralisation that presently characterises the federal system.

Chapter 6 focuses on issues related to increasing agitations in the period following the re-establishment of liberal democratic government in 1999 for a more functional federal system that fairly distributes the national wealth. There seems to be a consensus among political commentators that the practice of federalism in Nigeria does not conform to the fundamental principles of federalism because of the many conflicts within the system. This chapter, therefore, examines the mounting debate over 'true federalism' and 'restructuring', which have increasingly taken an ethno-regional dimension.

The final chapter presents the summary and conclusion of the book. Here, it is reiterated that Nigeria's domestic political economy entrenches over-dependency on oil and promotes over-centralisation of political and economic resources, and consequently, a flawed federal system. The book, therefore, recommends that the existing highly centralised federal system must give way to a decentralised system.

References

Abah, B. (2006, March/April). Nigeria Faces Conflict: Can Sharia Law Work in a Multi-religious Federation? *Federations: A Publication of the Forums of Federations*, 5(2), 3–4.

Aina, A. (1986). What Is Political Economy? In *The Nigerian Economy: A Political Economy Approach*. Essex: Longman Group.

Awa, E. (1976). *Issues in Federalism*. Benin City: Ethiope Publishing Corporation.

Ayoade, J. A. A. (1988, July). *Federalism in Nigeria: The Problem with the Solution*. Faculty Lecture Delivered at the University of Ibadan, Ibadan.

Baker, P. (1984). *The Economics of Nigerian Federalism*. Washington, DC: Battelle Memorial Institute.

Birch, A. (1955). *Federalism, Finance and Social Legislation in Canada, Australia and the United States*. Oxford: Clarendon Press.

Birch, A. (1966). Approaches to the Study of Federalism. *Political Studies, 14*, 15–33.

Burgess, M. (1993). Federalism and Federation: A Reappraisal. In M. Burgess & A.-G. Gagnon (Eds.), *Comparative Federalism and Federation: Competing Traditions and Future Directions*. New York and London: Harvester Wheatcheaf.

Burgess, M. (2006). *Comparative Federalism: Theory and Practice*. London and New York: Routledge.

Burgess, M. (2007). The British Tradition of Federalism: Nature, Meaning and Significance. In S. Henig (Ed.), *Federalism and the British*. London: Federal Trust.

Burgess, M. (2012a). *Federalism in Africa: An Essay on the Impacts of Cultural Diversity, Development and Democracy*. The Federal Idea: A Quebec Think Tank on Federalism.

Burgess, M. (2012b). *In Search of the Federal Spirit: New Theoretical and Empirical Perspectives in Comparative Federalism*. Oxford: Oxford University Press.

Dent, M. (2000). Nigeria: Federalism and Ethnic Rivalry. *Parliamentary Affairs, 53*, 157–168.

Diamond, L. (1988). *Class, Ethnicity and Democracy in Nigeria: The Failure of the First Republic*. London: Macmillan.

Dikshit, R. (1975). *The Political Geography of Federalism: An Enquiry into Origins and Stability*. New Delhi: Macmillan.

Duchacek, I. (1970). *Comparative Federalism: The Territorial Dimension of Politics, Lanham*. London: University Press of America.

Eatwell, J., Milgate, M., & Newman, P. (Eds.). (1987). *The New Palgrave Dictionary of Economics*. London and Basingstoke: Macmillan.

Elaigwu, J. (2007). *The Politics of Federalism in Nigeria*. London: Adonis & Abbey Publishers.

Elazar, D. (1973, Autumn). First Principles. *Publius: The Journal of Federalism, 3*(2), 1–10.

Elazar, D. (1987). *Exploring Federalism*. Tuscaloosa: The University of Alabama Press.

Friedrich, C. (1968). *Trends of Federalism in Theory and Practice*. New York: Praeger.

Horowitz, D. (2000). *Ethnic Groups in Conflict*. London: University of California Press.

Jinadu, A. (2016). The Federal Idea in Nigeria: From the Beginnings to 1946. In O. Ibeanu & M. J. Kuna (Eds.), *Nigerian Federalism: Continuing Quest for Stability and Nation-Building*. Ibadan: Safari Books.
King, P. (1982). *Federalism and Federation*. Baltimore: Johns Hopkins University Press.
Kirk-Greene, A. H. M. (1967). The Peoples of Nigeria: The Cultural Background to the Crisis. *African Affairs, 262*, 3–11.
Livingston, W. (1952). A Note on the Nature of Federalism. *Political Science Quarterly*, *67*, 81–95.
Livingston, W. (1956). *Federalism and Constitutional Change*. Oxford: Clarendon Press.
Macmahon, A. (1962). The Problems of Federalism: A Survey. In A. Macmahon (Ed.), *Federalism: Mature and Emergent*. New York: Russell & Russell.
Macmahon, A. (1972). *Administering Federalism in a Democracy*. New York: Oxford University Press.
Nnoli, O. (1995). *Ethnicity and Development in Nigeria*. Aldershot: Avebury.
Nolte, I. (2002, Spring). Federalism and Communal Conflict in Nigeria. *Regional and Federal Studies*, *12*(1), 171–192.
Riker, W. (1964). *Federalism: Origin, Operation, Significance*. Boston: Little, Brown.
Sawer, G. (1969). *Modern Federalism*. London: C. A. Watts & Co.
Stepan, A. (1999). Federalism and Democracy: Beyond the US Model. *Journal of Democracy*, *10*(4), 19–34.
Suberu, R. (2001). *Federalism and Ethnic Conflict in Nigeria*. Washington, DC: United States Institute of Peace Press.
Verney, D. (1995). Federalism, Federative Systems, and Federations: The United States, Canada, and India. *Publius: The Journal of Federalism*, *25*(2), 81–97.
Watts, R. (1966). *New Federations: Experiments in the Commonwealth*. Oxford: Clarendon Press.
Wheare, K. (1963). *Federal Government* (4th ed.). London: Oxford University Press.
Wheare, K. (1968). *Legislatures*. London: Oxford University Press.
Williams, G. (Ed.). (1976). *Nigeria: Economy and Society*. London: Rex Collings.

CHAPTER 2

Nigeria, a Federal State and Federal Society: The Origins

Introduction

This chapter focuses primarily on the origin of the Nigerian federation, as well as the nature of the federal society. A deep understanding of the workings of Nigeria's federal system may not be possible without some understanding of its origin and the character of the society. Scholars of federalism have emphasised the causal relationship between the origin and success or failure of a federation (Hicks 1978, p. 5; Stepan 2001, p. 320). Given the political salience of ethnicity, religion, and other social forces, both in the creation of federations and the operation of federalism, the societal aspect of the institutional structure should be given the attention it deserves. If we concur that the essential characteristics of federalism are not only about the constitutional division of powers but also about the society, then our study of Nigeria's federal political system must not be limited to the question of institutional structure, neither must it be limited to the social forces inherent in the federation, but rather to the interplay of the two.

Examining the origin of the Nigerian federation provides an insight into those centripetal and centrifugal forces that coalesced to give rise to the federation and how these forces impact on the operation of federalism in the country. Different explanations have been offered regarding the factors that induce federations in general. For convenience, we try to subsume these explanations under two perspectives: the socio-economic

D. Babalola, *The Political Economy of Federalism in Nigeria*, Federalism and Internal Conflicts,
https://doi.org/10.1007/978-3-030-05493-9_2

perspective, which argues that federations come into being as a result of the presence of certain social and economic conditions; and the political perspective, which points to the presence of some political factors.

The origin of the Nigerian federation has, likewise, elicited two contrasting perspectives, with some scholars arguing that the country's pre-colonial structures, extensive geographical size, ethnic diversity and economic variations were the underlying factors that have made federalism almost inevitable (Awa 1964, 1976; Ayoade 1973; Birch 1966; Elaigwu 2007; Suberu 2001; Watts 1966). Others have, however, rejected these views and have argued that the British colonialists deliberately imposed federalism on Nigeria in order to maintain a neo-colonial control of the state after their departure. The crux of this latter argument is that the British calculatingly left behind some structural weaknesses that would provide them with an opportunity to continue to interfere in the internal affairs of the former colony (Afigbo 1991; Eleazu 1977; Osuntokun 1979; Oyovbaire 1983, 1985). These viewpoints, as divergent as they seem, are interwoven, but an attempt is made to synthesise them with a view to unravelling the roots of the oldest federation in Africa. In doing so, we argue that the social heterogeneity of Nigeria made federalism the most appropriate political framework for the country. The starting point, therefore, is, to begin with an examination of the various perspectives on federal formations.

Origin of Federations: A Socio-economic Perspective

The socio-economic perspective of the origin of federalism holds that a federal system of government is a response to certain social and economic conditions. There is no better place, therefore, to start the exploration of this viewpoint than the influential work of the doyen of federalism, Kenneth C. Wheare titled, *Federal Government*. In that seminal work, Wheare pointed out that, certain political, social and economic factors conjoined to bring about the formation of the Federation of Australia, Canada, Switzerland and the United States. These factors are worth reproducing here in detail:

> A sense of military insecurity and of the consequent need for common defence; a desire to be independent of foreign powers, and a realisation that only through union could independence be secured; a hope of economic advantage from union; some political association of the communities concerned prior to their federal union…; geographical neighbourhood; and similarity of political institutions. (1963, p. 37)

For Wheare, whilst these 'prerequisites' are significant, even more, significant is the desire to form a federal union. The point here is that the presence of these conditions does not automatically translate into a federation; there must be a desire on the part of the political elites to form a union. In other words, the main driving force behind the formation of a federation is the willingness or desire of states or communities to come together for certain purposes. That is, they must desire to be united and not to be unitary (Wheare 1963, p. 36). What is essential, therefore, in Wheare's view is the desire of the leaders of the territories concerned to be within one big political unit. Following on from Wheare, Karl Deutsch and his research collaborators also emphasised the relevance of the socio-economic conditions.

Similarly, armed with findings from his empirical study of the six 'new federations' of India, Malaysia, Nigeria, Pakistan, Rhodesia and Nyasaland, and the West Indies, Watts (1966, p. 66) also argued that the impact of political, social, cultural, economic and historical factors cannot be overemphasised in the formation of the modern federations, but the necessity of common defence, as alluded to by Wheare, was significant only in the Asian federations. He argued further that unlike in the 'old federations' of Australia, Canada, Switzerland and the United States, the motives for a union in the developing countries are more complex. Nonetheless, such other factors for unity usually present in the old federations (established federal states) are also present in the new federations and often lead to a desire for union. According to Watts, the following eleven factors are essential to the formation of a federal union:

> The desire for political independence; the hope of economic advantage; the need for administrative efficiency; the enhancing of the conduct of external relations, both diplomatic and military; a community of outlook based on race, religion, language, or culture; geographical factors; the influence of history; similarities and differences in colonial and indigenous political and social institutions; the character of political leadership; the existence of successful older models of federal union; and the influence of the United Kingdom government in constitution-making. (Watts 1966, p. 42)

Each of these factors is potentially either 'centripetal or centrifugal', that is, 'unifying or separating' (Davis 1978, p. 128; Watts 1966, p. 42; Wheare 1963, p. 40). In other words, some of the factors are forces for unity, while others are forces for disintegration. Watts concluded his survey of the new federations by highlighting the two main features common to them all as regards federal formation: a geographical distribution of the diversities within each of these societies, which results in the demands for regional political autonomy; and the existence of some form of desire to be united (Watts 1966, p. 93). We shall return to these features when we discuss the formation of the Nigerian federation.

The main theme in these scholars' viewpoints is that the presence of social and economic factors, as well the desire to form a union, cannot be ignored in the formation of federations. The notion of the desire to be united, as observed by Wheare and reinforced by Watts, has, however, come under criticism by Davis (1978, p. 141), who questioned how possible it is to measure a 'balance of desire'. He was of the view that '[a] theory of federal parturition relying on a balance of ambivalent desires' cannot explain why federal unions are formed. But in support of Watts' position is Burgess (2006, p. 81), who argued that 'analytically, there is a two-step process involved in the creation of a federation: the first is the desire for union while the second is the decision to have a federal union'. Burgess's argument is predicated upon his study of the federations of Australia, Austria, Canada, India, Germany, Malaysia and Switzerland.

Origin of Federations: A Political Perspective

Of all the works on the political theory of federal formation, the one that has attracted the most attention is William H. Riker's *Federalism: Origin, Operation, Significance* originally published in 1964. Riker made no pretence about his effort to develop a political science that would provide 'testable and tested generalisations'. It is, therefore, pertinent to begin with Riker's idea of federalism, as this may provide an insight into his theory of federal formation. He defined federalism 'as a bargain between prospective national leaders and officials of constituent governments' usually for the purpose of achieving the objectives of aggregating territory, laying taxes and raising armies (Riker 1964, p. 11). Logically, Riker's notion of federal origin is predicated upon the assumption that federalism is an outcome of political bargaining among rational politicians, and implicit in this definition is that the bargain is like a contract involving some offer and acceptance. Moreover, the 'rational' politicians making the offer must be convinced of the benefits derivable from the proposed union, while their counterparts accepting the offer would also have to be convinced that the advantages of belonging to a union outweigh the disadvantages. So why do elites make such an offer and why do their counterparts accept the offer?

Riker's theory is built upon a two-fold condition, the expansion condition and the military condition, both of which are *always* present in the federal bargain and each is *necessary* for the formation of a federation. In other words, these two conditions were present in virtually all federations including India, Malaysia and Nigeria, which, according to Riker, share a common characteristic in regards to their formation. Riker began the formulation of his theory by bluntly dismissing as 'ideological fallacy' the idea that federalism was adopted as a guarantee of freedom, and the idea that it was formed among polities that hold a common interest as 'reductionist fallacy' (Riker 1964, pp. 13–15). This criticism was based on his view that the ideas precluded the political aspect of federal formation—a political bargain between two sets of politicians. The following more aptly presents Riker's argument, particularly against Deutsch's nine 'essential conditions' referred to earlier: 'In bypassing the political, in bypassing the act of bargaining itself, it leaves out the crucial condition of the predisposition to make the bargain' (Riker 1964, p. 16). Riker went further to contend that the list only provides a set of frequently observed conditions that propel politicians towards a predisposition to unite in some way or another. Thus, in Riker's opinion, earlier ideas on the formation of a federation are ideological rather than scientific.

Now let us authenticate Riker's claim within some of the federations he studied, beginning with Australia. Here, he conceded that economic factors cannot be completely ignored in the formation of the federation, and also that there was no immediate threat when the federation was formed. He, however, pointed out that the presence of some 'military-diplomatic concerns' informed the decision taken by the founders of the country. The two main claims made by Riker regarding Australia can be summarised thus: that the formation of the federation was precipitated by the fear of Japanese imperialism in East Asia, and that because these threats were relatively weak it was necessary only to create a peripheralised federation that reflected the strength of provincial as opposed to national loyalties (Riker 1964, p. 27).

In the case of India, Riker posited that the formation of its federation was occasioned by external threats from Pakistan, which was 'more warlike, better armed, and more resentful', and internal threats from the princely states, which were 'a collection of partially self-governing colonies in 1947' (Riker 1964, p. 29). Despite recognising the influence of the colonial constitutional engineering that culminated in the formation of the federation, particularly the influence of *The Government of India*

Act of 1935, he still preferred to argue that the two forms of threat earlier mentioned combined to give birth to the federation.

For Malaysia, Riker asserted authoritatively that the formation of the federation fulfilled his hypothesis in the sense that the military condition was present and was evidenced in the existence of communist guerrillas, supported by China, while the expansion condition was also present due to the need to reconcile the previously federated states. He declared with certainty that, 'the motive for this federalism was 'a fear of Indonesian imperialism and a reluctance, on the part of Singapore, Borneo, and others to accept Malayan domination' (Riker 1964, p. 31).

As regards the formation of the Nigerian federation, Riker argued that the main external threat that influenced the formation of the federation was the expansionist ambition of Ghana and its then leader, Kwame Nkrumah. Arguing further, Riker contended that Nkrumah's spirit of Pan-Africanism was so high that 'no Nigerian leader could fail to be aware of the proximity of the Western (and depressed and minority) region of Nigeria to Ghana' (pp. 31–32). The main internal threat, he argued, was 'the unwillingness of Nigerian leaders to upset the bargain the British had made for them' (Riker 1964, pp. 31–32). The point Riker was making here is that the combination of these threats influenced the British to pave the way for the federation. As the British withdrawal became imminent, argued Riker, the British split the country into three parts in anticipation of a future federation, and the justification for doing so was the existence of three geographically distinct and politically hostile cultures within the colony, which later formed themselves into a union. Clearly, Riker did not let the significance of Nigeria's cultural diversity escape him in his analysis. It is therefore interesting that he nonetheless attributed the formation of the federation to the fear of insecurity posed by Ghana.

The postulation that the Nigerian federation was necessitated by an external threat from Ghana has, however, been discountenanced by scholars conversant with the political history of Nigeria. Anthony Birch, for example, had noted that the Western Region of Nigeria, which Riker described as 'depressed', was, in fact, the most prosperous of the three Nigerian Regions, and the federal idea in Nigeria was conceived while Nkrumah was still in the United States studying. He argued further that, besides, most Nigerian leaders shared, to varying degrees, the Pan-African ideology (Birch 1966, p. 23; Eleazu 1977, p. 18).

Riker may be right in arguing that the fear of conquest by an external power can induce territories to form themselves into a single federal state, but this argument in relation to Nigeria is unsustainable. The threat criterion is unfounded and the argument paints a picture of someone who either misunderstood or misinterpreted Nigerian political history. Some threats might have contributed to inducing Nigeria's federal union, but contrary to Riker's assertion, these threats were internal from the regions within the country and not from outside. As a matter of fact, the French neighbouring countries posed no threat of any sort to Nigeria. The palpable fear and suspicion of domination among the different ethnic groups reinforced the colonial authority's calculation to promote the idea of federalism (Awa 1976, p. 19; Birch 1966, p. 25; Elaigwu 2007, p. 22). So, Riker's theory should have also accommodated an internal threat from prospective partners in the federation. After all, he acknowledged the presence of three 'hostile cultures within the colony'. Perhaps this could have saved him from the scathing criticism that his work belonged to the 'quasi-scientific style of the behavioural movement', aspiring to transcend the 'unique' historical and cultural setting of each federal experience to establish 'tested and testable generalisation' (Davis 1978, pp. 125–126). As shall be shown later, decades after the formation of the Nigerian federation, each ethnic group continues to live in fear of being marginalised.

Having studied the federations of Austria and West Germany, Ramesh Dikshit (1975) also posited that Riker's so-called necessary conditions were not necessary to the formation of federations. Dikshit argued further that Riker was neither the first nor the only scholar to point out the importance of a military condition or external threat or the expansion condition. This position, he argued had earlier been articulated by scholars such as William Maddox, H. R. G. Greaves and K. C. Wheare (p. 223). Indeed, Maddox (1941, p. 1122) had earlier observed that some of the motivations behind the formation of federations are fear, a calculated expectation of advantage and a response to some unifying ideal or myth, but fear that may develop from direct attempts at intimidation, or from a sustained and profound feeling of insecurity is the most important of these political or psychological forces.

Also critical of Riker's account of federal formation is Davis (1978), who argued that all unions are formed, in the first place, with the primary desire to promote the well-being of their members. So, security becomes the underlying motive in the calculation to form a federal union. For Davis (1978, p. 133), therefore, there is nothing innovative in recognising the security motive in the formation of a federal union, because it is to be expected 'that every writer would note the presence of this factor in the list of motives for federal union'. Another critic of Riker's idea of federal formation is King (1982, pp. 35–36), who observed that it is obvious that, to every state, there is always some risk of external war and domestic dissension, and that the source of risk is three-fold: threat to a particular state from within the state; threat to one state from another state; and threat to allied states from another state. In other words, a threat from within the state may provoke that state to form a union just like a threat to one state from another may provoke a federation between them. According to King, the internal threat appears to have been the case with the federations of Nigeria, Switzerland and the United States. The crux of King's argument is that if the birth of a federation is predicated upon the fear of other powers, then any type of fear must provide grounds for a federal union; hence, Riker's 'threat' criterion makes generalisation difficult.

Some scholars are, however, less critical of Riker's theory. Notable among Riker's sympathisers is David McKay, who, though, conceded that Riker's exclusion of the social and economic conditions is too restrictive because these factors are equally important to the federal formation. McKay, however, went on to argue that Riker's theory cannot simply be flawed on the ground that all countries actually or potentially face threats as claimed by critics. For McKay (2004, p. 170), therefore, external threats may lead to annexation, treaty or war and/or federation, especially when certain special conditions are met, and the level of threat will determine the particular arrangements arrived at.

Origin of Federations: New Perspectives

The intellectual debate on federal formation was joined by Alfred Stepan, who chose to examine the modes of federal creation rather than the factors that result in federations. Firstly, he criticised Riker for focusing exclusively on the American Federation, which represents the oldest and the most successful federation in the world. Secondly, he simplified the argument in his oft-cited typology that helps to explain that federations are formed in three major ways: coming together; holding together; and putting together (Stepan 1999). Australia, Switzerland and the United States are referred to as 'coming together' federations. This is because previously sovereign units pool their sovereignties while retaining their individual identities (p. 21). Whereas, a 'holding together' federation is formed when an existing unitary state, usually characterised by 'historical and political logic', metamorphoses into a federation (p. 21). India and Nigeria exemplify a 'holding together' federation. The reason for this is that both were unitary states before becoming federations. Moreover, each lacked bargaining between sovereign states, as the constituent units were not sovereign in the same sense as the American states that united. Finally, a 'putting together' federation is that which involves the use of coercion to put together previously independent states (p. 23). An example was the defunct Soviet Union. According to Stepan, Georgia, Azerbaijan, and Armenia were independent states before their conquest by the 11th Red Army. Of significant note is that the use of force is obvious in the case of a 'putting together' federation.

Stepan's theoretical framework is thought-provoking, especially when one considers the processes involved in the creation of a federation like Nigeria. What seems unclear, however, is where to locate a country like Russia, which was part of the defunct USSR but emerged as a federation in 1993, when the Soviet Union collapsed. The present-day Russian federation was neither put together by force nor was it originally a unitary state. Furthermore, it may be argued that Stepan is echoing Maddox's views, who had earlier contended that a federation may develop either from a centrifugal force—the breaking down of a unitary form of government; or from centripetal force—the building up of parts into a new entity (Maddox 1941, p. 1121).

Also worth discussing are the new federal models that emerged in the post-Cold War era. Federations in this latest category are typically multinational in character and have come into being as a result of external pressures. As part of state-building projects, international actors have promoted the federal idea for countries facing an internal conflict between territorially-based groups. These states have been referred to as 'forced together' or 'imposed' federations because they owe their creations to the vagaries of the international community (Burgess 2012, p. 304; Keil 2013; Shakir 2017). In each of them, federalism was adopted as a tool for conflict resolution. Although the states are products of post-conflict state-building processes, the existence of diversity in terms of religion and ethnicity cannot be ruled out in the calculation to form a union. Three states stand out here: Bosnia and Herzegovina (BiH); Ethiopia and Iraq. Let us examine the formation of these federations, in brief, beginning with Ethiopia.

Modern-day Ethiopia is the second largest country in Africa, with a population of about 90 million and over eighty different ethnic groups. There are about ninety different languages spoken across the country. Ethiopia used to be characterised by serious ethnic tensions until 1991 when the civil war that lasted for seventeen years came to an end. This also brought about the fall of the then military regime (Dergue), as well as the rise of the Ethiopian Peoples' Revolutionary Democratic Front (EPRDF). This political organisation comprises a number of ethnically based opposition groups, which sought a political framework that would guarantee the accommodation of diversity inherent in the Ethiopian society. After a series of negotiations, overseen by the United States in particular, a federal solution was agreed upon in 1995. The emergent federation, organised along the lines of ethnically based constituent units, was aimed at achieving ethnic and regional autonomy, whilst at the same time maintaining the state of Ethiopia as a political unit (Habtu 2005, p. 313; Keller 2002, p. 21). Although some form of external influence contributed to the establishment of the federation, it must be said that the federal state also fits into Stepan's typology of a 'holding together' federation, because it was a product of elite compromise aimed at reducing ethnic conflict.

BiH is another multinational federation that seems to fit the recent classification of a 'forced together' or 'imposed' federation. Like the Ethiopian federation, BiH arose out of a civil war between Bosnian Serbs, Bosnian Croatians and Bosniaks (i.e. Muslims) to become a federation in 1995. The Dayton Peace Agreement of that year laid the basis for the reconstruction of the new federal state. The federal solution was not an outcome of a voluntary agreement between the former warring parties, but an imposition by the international community comprising the United Nations (UN), the North Atlantic Treaty Organisation (NATO), the European Union (EU) and the Organisation for Security and Cooperation in Europe (OSCE) (Burgess 2012, pp. 299–305; Keil 2013; Woelk 2004, pp. 177–198). According to Keil (2013, p. 4), the international community intervened to help resolve the conflict that had ravaged Bosnia and so Bosnia and Herzegovina became the first state to experience a new model of federalism, namely 'imposed federalism' and a new model of a federal state, that of the 'internationally administered federation'. Nonetheless, since the federation was formed as a panacea to ethnic tension, we might as well say that it is a 'holding together' federation.

Similar to BiH is the Iraqi federation, which also emerged as a post-conflict compromise. The federation was the outcome of regime change spearheaded by the United States and the United Kingdom in 2003 rather than an arrangement by the international community in the real sense of the word (Shakir 2017). That said, the role of the international community in the federalising process cannot be overstated. Like Ethiopia and BiH, Iraq may be viewed from the perspective of a 'holding together' federation simply because the aim was to have a state capable of holding together the different religious groups in the country.

Origin of the Nigerian Federation: The Socio-Economic Perspective

One significant account of Nigeria's federal formation is that of Anthony Birch, whose analysis of Nigerian politics, in general, would seem reasonably coherent given his knowledge of the country.[1] He argued that, of the nine conditions postulated by Deutsch and his colleagues, the following four constituted the motives for Nigeria's federal union: expectations of stronger economic ties or gains; a marked increase in political and administrative capabilities of at least some participating units; superior economic growth on the part of at least some participating units; and a multiplicity of ranges of communications and transactions. Moreover, he asserted that the last four of Wheare's conditions (as highlighted above)—a hope of economic advantage from union; some previous political association; geographical neighbourhood; and similarity of political institutions—were present, but the first condition, that is, a sense of military insecurity and the consequent need for common defence, was absent because there was no outside military threat to Nigeria, thus the need for a common defence was unnecessary (Birch 1966, p. 23).

Birch was right in making reference to the presence of these factors, but his exclusion of Wheare's second condition, that is, the desire for political independence—a factor Watts described as one of the most important motives for an inter-territorial union, particularly in the new federations—has rendered his analysis incomplete. The story of federalism in Nigeria will not be complete without paying attention to the

[1]Anthony Birch acted as a consultant to the Western Region government from 1956 to 1958. Although, it could be said that this was after the introduction of federalism yet his knowledge of the country cannot be overstated.

regional leaders' desire for independence from the British colonialists. Economic interdependence, the desire to achieve political interdependence and the effect of common British rule, no doubt, constituted the unifying motives for a union, whilst the vast size of the country and its inbuilt ethnic and cultural diversity were the variables of disunity. Ethnic and cultural factors, for example, may exert a negative influence in the sense that people of dissimilar ethnic and cultural backgrounds may see themselves as incompatible but may desire union for the sake of other advantages. But as we shall show shortly, the centripetal (unifying) forces were dominant in the calculation to transform the previously unitary state into a federation. In what follows, we examine each of these motives.

The desire to achieve political independence from the British imperial power and the fervent belief that only through unity could this be possible cannot be ruled out in the quest of Nigeria's elites for a federal political framework (Watts 1966, p. 43). During the struggle for decolonisation, the elites were always quick to highlight the need for unity in the interest of achieving independence. They gave their followers the impression that the British government would not accede to the nationalists' demand for independence unless they were united.

Furthermore, scholars in favour of the economic premise for federation hinge their argument on the belief that a federal union brings about a strong financial base, which, if properly managed, can translate into administrative efficiency. Just like in the Canadian case, the architects of Nigeria's federal union had hoped that the pooling of economic resources from various territories would lead to a large internal market. Moreover, forming a union would afford the poorer territories to benefit from the wealthier ones. The impact of complementary regional economies on inducing union is, in fact, illustrated by the Nigerian federation, where differences in climate, soil and food crops played a decisive role (Watts 1966, p. 49). Putting this more precisely is Ayoade (1973, p. 60), who argued that the mono-crop economy of the East (palm produce), the West (cocoa) and the North (groundnut) made a federal solution advisable. In addition to this, the Eastern Region was a large reservoir of unskilled, semi-skilled and skilled labour; the Northern Region was also rich in cotton, hides and skins, while the Western Region also had a large reservoir of professionals and bureaucrats (Awa 1976, p. 25). The development under British rule of interdependent economies helped to pave the way for the desire for union. It also contributed, in no small measure, to the success of the federation in the immediate post-independence period, when the constituent units enjoyed significant fiscal autonomy.

It has also been established that geographical contiguity, that is, the nearness of people to one another, was a feature common in all the established federations at the time of their formation, and likewise the new federations of India, Malaysia and Nigeria (Watts 1966, pp. 55–57). Given the sheer size of Nigeria, it would have been difficult for a single authority to address the differing complex needs of the people located in various parts of the country. The British administrators were able to link the colonial administrative units through railway networks, roads and telecommunications, thereby bringing about some ties amongst the peoples. This enabled the elites to harness the resources of the different territories with the hope of developing a large market (Awa 1976, p. 16).

Another factor that produced a desire for union among the territories that formed themselves into a union in Nigeria is the historical impact of British rule. Prior to unification, all regions in the country, despite their differences, shared similar political and social institutions, as well as some unifying historical forces such as inter-territorial political association. The similarity in the administrative system and a shared *lingua franca* combined to induce a desire for union. These similarities were not a mere coincidence and they preceded the federation. The British colonial policy after the Second World War favoured closer territorial association in their colonies, as well as a policy of unification (Watts 1966, pp. 62–65). These generated in the leaders a desire to unite for some purposes.

Likewise, the ethnic and cultural factors that characterised the Nigerian society induced in the peoples of the different territories a desire for federal union (Awa 1976, pp. 26–30; Elaigwu 2007, p. 32; Suberu 2001, pp. 19–21; 2004, p. 330). According to Suberu (2004, p. 330), the decision to federalise the hitherto unitary state could be traced to 'the country's deep cultural fragmentation and the aggravation of this diversity by sundry colonial policies'. The British promoted the federal idea in Nigeria having come to the realisation that the differences among the Nigerian peoples could only be accommodated in a federation. Thus, the decision to transform the country into a federal state was partly borne out of the country's multi-ethnicity.

For the student of the socio-economic school, therefore, the desire to achieve independence, the hope of economic advantage, ethnic and cultural diversity and the impact of British rule were all potent forces for a federal political framework in Nigeria.

Origin of the Nigerian Federation: The Colonial Legacy Perspective

The relevance of the socio-economic factors to the formation of the Nigerian federation has been dismissed by scholars, who argued that the British imposed a federal system of government on the peoples of Nigeria. These scholars are always quick to point to the gradual political process involved in bringing the territory, now known as Nigeria, together as a colony. Arguing with great subtlety, Afigbo (1991), for instance, asserted that the geographic size and ecological diversity of Nigeria played no part in the formation of the federation because the federation has never at any point in its history been a federation of natural, geographic, economic regions; rather, these factors only influenced the allocation of responsibilities between the centre and the federating units. He argued further that, 'the geographic and economic configuration of Nigeria cannot be used to make a strong case for any particular government arrangement—unitary, federal, or confederal' (p. 17). Another argument against the socio-economic standpoint is that the pre-colonial structures were irrelevant because, historically, the 'federated units' did not have a separate existence as political systems prior to the colonial presence, when 'Nigeria' did not exist (Oyovbaire 1985, p. 17).

Central to the colonial legacy thesis is that the impact of British rule on the formation of the Nigerian federation is real and significant. British colonial rule in Nigeria began with the annexation of Lagos in 1861. In 1900 the British formally took over direct control of the area that was until then under the Royal Niger Company (RNC) and declared it the Protectorate of Northern Nigeria, whilst the Protectorate of Southern Nigeria and the Colony of Lagos operated as separate administrative units. Nigeria remained a single colonial territory but with three distinct administrative blocks. Each administrative unit was allowed to operate a system of administration that suited the needs of the people of that territory. The colony of Nigeria was administered as three separate political units until 1906, when the Protectorate of Southern Nigeria and the Colony of Lagos were brought under single administrative control, thereby creating two administrations—Northern and Southern.

In 1914 the Northern and the Southern Protectorates were amalgamated by the then colonial governor, Sir Frederick Lugard. It is important to stress that this action did not result from pressure of any sort from Nigerian peoples but for reasons of administrative convenience.

The emphasis was on 'the immediate problems and their solution at minimum cost', as well as Lugard's 'personal convenience and working habits' (Ballard 1971, pp. 334–335). There was a shortage of funds and of British officials to run the colony and the colonial administrators were not prepared to use the resources from the mother-country to run their colonies. The resultant effect was two separate administrative policies in one country, one for the Northern protectorate and the other for the Southern protectorate, making Nigeria a unitary state with two distinct territorial administrations. One major implication of this policy of duality was that it did not encourage horizontal interactions among the peoples of these two separate areas. This was to later result in contemptuous, distrustful and antagonistic behaviour among the peoples that have been brought together in one large political unit.

In 1939 the then colonial governor, Sir Bernard Bourdillon, in what seemed to be a recognition of the three 'natural' regions in the country—north, west and east—split Southern Nigeria into the Western and Eastern Regions, apparently for administrative efficiency. This constitutional arrangement was equally recognised by Bourdillon's successor, Sir Arthur Richards, who ensured its entrenchment in the Nigerian Constitution of 1946. It is interesting to note that these three administrative units were to later form the basic building blocks of the Nigerian federal structure. Nonetheless, scholars of the colonial legacy persuasion maintain that each of them came into being purely for reasons of administrative convenience rather than a consideration to maintain the integrity of geographic, cultural and/or linguistic areas (Afigbo 1991, p. 17; Oyovbaire 1985, p. 35). The 1946 Constitution provided a platform for political interaction from the two geographical divides. For the first time, elites from both sides participated in the affairs of the country in a central legislative House. Despite the interactions between the two sets of elites, there was still a high degree of distrust, with each feeling more comfortable in their respective ethno-regional cocoon.

These interactions were manifest in the series of conferences that led to the emergence of a federal constitution in 1954. The Ibadan constitutional conference of 1950, for instance, gave birth to the Macpherson Constitution of 1951, which changed the status of the three main administrative units into 'Regions' with enhanced political and financial autonomy. This Constitution introduced limited federalism, or what has been referred to as 'quasi-federalism' because the central government still possessed powers of control over the Regions. Technically, therefore, the Constitution was unitary in character, as the Regions were short of possessing full autonomy.

In August 1953 a conference was held in London in which Nigerian political leaders met with the representatives of the British government to discuss the defects of the 1951 quasi-federal constitution, as well as the question of self-government in 1956. Earlier that year, Anthony Enahoro, a parliamentarian from the Western Region, moved a motion for 'self-government in 1956' in the national parliament, but delegates from the North, through Sir Ahmadu Bello moved the adoption of an amendment replacing the words 'in 1956' with 'as soon as practicable', and even threatened to pull out of the federal project because the Region did 'not want to be stampeded into self-rule' (Coleman 1958, p. 399). This conference was inconclusive, as the leaders failed to agree on the knotty issues of when to achieve independence, and the status of Lagos, among other things.

On the status of Lagos, the Yoruba-dominated Action Group (AG), representing the Western Region wanted Lagos to be part of the Western Region, as was the case under the 1951 Constitution. Their argument was predicated upon administrative convenience (Awa 1964, p. 52). They threatened to pull out of the negotiation for a federal solution if this was not agreed (Ayoade 1973, p. 68). The Eastern delegates, however, maintained that Lagos had been developed at the expense of the whole country and should remain the federal capital. The Northern delegates also argued that the port facilities in Lagos made the city the economic lifeline of the entire country and that its merger with the Western Region would mean a loss of access to the sea if the West should secede. The Yoruba leaders were quick to point out that Lagos was primarily a Yoruba town situated in the western part of the country, and as such, a new capital should be built in the event of the Nigerian state becoming a federation. Surprisingly, the Colonial Secretary, Sir Oliver Lyttleton issued a strong warning to the Western Region delegates saying:

> any attempt to secure alteration of that decision by force will be resisted, and in this context, I am to observe that any attempt to secure the secession of the Western Region from the Federation would be regarded as the use of force. (Quoted in Ayoade 1973, p. 68)

With this threat from the British government, Obafemi Awolowo and other Yoruba leaders were compelled to jettison the threat of secession.

Another conference had to be held in Lagos in January and February 1954, and this time, a federal form of government in which the Regions were accorded full autonomy was entrenched, and Lagos assumed a separate status as the federal capital. Another important compromise that was made in the 1954 conference was that the Southern Regions' demand for self-government in 1956 was granted, whilst the North, whose leaders argued that it was not ready for such, was also allowed to attain the same, albeit later than the others in 1959. The Northern delegates had insisted that if self-government were to come, they must be accorded a separate state. However, they agreed to consider joining in a federation with the peoples of the other two Regions after extensive negotiations (Wheare 1962, p. 31). The Federal Constitution was named after Sir Oliver Lyttleton, the then British Colonial Secretary. By 1954 Nigeria emerged as a federation of three constituent units, namely, the Northern Region, the Western Region and the Eastern Region.

The Nigerian Federation: An Imposition or a Desire?

We have found it more useful to see the perspectives discussed thus far as mutually reinforcing. After all, we have been reminded that the mere presence of social and economic conditions in a given territory will not in itself lead to a desire to unite. A great deal depends on political leadership because federations are based on negotiations and compromises, which require strong leadership. The American federation, despite the presence of social and economic conditions, was made possible due to the leadership quality displayed by the country's founding fathers, namely, Washington, Hamilton, Jay and Madison, and their desire to unite the American colonies (Wheare 1963, p. 31). Similarly, the influence and charismatic leadership of Nehru and Gandhi played a significant part in the formation of the Indian Federation (Watts 1966, p. 61). Although Nigeria could not boast of similar national political leaders, its regional leaders, using their ethno-regional political parties as platforms, exerted a great deal of influence over their followers as they promoted the federal idea. The country's founding fathers, based on their desire for union, jettisoned their differences to arrive at a federal compromise after some laborious negotiations.

There is no denying that the British colonial rule played a part in the adoption of a federal system in Nigeria but the impact of the country's diversity, as well as the desire on the part of the leaders, should also not be ignored. During the struggle for decolonisation, Nigerian regional leaders actively collaborated with the British colonial authorities to promote the federal idea. Nnamdi Azikiwe and his Igbo-dominated National Council of Nigerian Citizens (NCNC), representing the Eastern Region, and Obafemi Awolowo, leader of the Yoruba-dominated Action Group (AG), similarly representing the Western Region, particularly favoured the federal idea, believing that the system would promote unity in diversity. Ahmadu Bello, leader of the Hausa-Fulani-dominated Northern People's Congress (NPC), also believed that a federal political arrangement was the 'only guarantee that the country will progress evenly all over, for we can spend the money we receive, the money we raise, in the direction best suited to us' (Bello 1962, p. 18). Azikiwe had, in his book, *Political Blueprint of Nigeria*, published in 1943, envisaged a federal Nigeria, made up of eight component units or 'protectorates' based on ethnic affiliation (cited in Awa 1964, p. 25), while Awolowo also used his book, *Path to Nigerian Freedom*, published in 1947, to argue that only a federal system, based on the ten main ethnic groupings in the country, would suit Nigeria's political conditions (p. 48). The number of constituent units advocated notwithstanding, the main point of convergence here is that Nigerian elites desired federalism.

An indication that the adoption of federalism in Nigeria was negotiated, agreed and welcomed by all regional leaders emerged when Dr. Nnamdi Azikwe, who became a member of the federal House of Representatives in 1954, remarked that 'as for me and those who think like me politically, we are determined to make the revised constitution an avenue for holding the country together through a strong federal government' (NAI, NL/H2 Nigeria, House of Representatives Debates, Third Session, March 8, 1954, p. 37, quoted in Osadolor 1998, p. 43). By 'revised constitution', Azikwe meant the 1954 Federal Constitution. The statement also implied that the purpose of federalism in the multi-ethnic state was to hold the country together. In a similar vein, the country's first prime minister, Sir Abubakar Tafawa Balewa, commented in the federal House of Representatives in 1957 that:

> I am pleased to see that *we have all agreed* that the federal system is, under the present conditions, the only sure basis on which Nigeria can remain united. We must recognise our diversity and the peculiar conditions under which the different tribal communities live in this country. To us, in

> Nigeria, therefore, unity in diversity is a source of great strength, and we must do all in our power to see that this federal system of government is strengthened and maintained. (Balewa 1964, p. 2. Emphasis added)

It is clear from the above statements that all the country's political leaders undeniably agreed on a federal solution. However, scholars sympathetic to the imposition thesis have maintained that the ensued federation was neither a 'contract' between states nor a voluntary union of a number of originally independent states, but rather a political development from an amalgam of unitary colonial structures (Oyovbaire 1985, p. 17). This school's rejection of social and economic conditions in the formation of the federation and its exclusive focus on political conditions seems a one-dimensional argument. Of course, there was no 'contract' between hitherto independent states, but there were negotiations and concessions between Nigerian regional political leaders. We are also aware that the formation of the federation did not follow the same process as that of the United States, in which hitherto independent states agreed to unite for some purposes. Nonetheless, it is important to acknowledge that Nigeria's federal system resulted from a consensus decision reached by Nigeria's elites.

All these points considered, conceiving Nigeria's federation as an imposition underplays the significance of the degree of diversity in the country, as well as the contributions made by the country's political elites. The willingness or desire of the country's founding fathers to unite the different territories under a single political umbrella, principally for some social and economic considerations cannot be ignored. This attests to the view that federation is a child of compromise, equilibrium or a balance between centripetal and centrifugal forces. The question, therefore, is: why did the political leaders opt for a federal political system as the only basis upon which Nigeria could remain united? Generally, elites do favour the federal idea, as Burgess (1999, p. 1) has argued, because federations 'have the institutional and structural capacity both to accommodate and reconcile different forms of unity with different forms of diversity.'

Federalism may mean different things to the founding fathers of Nigeria, but there seems to be a point of convergence. For Azikwe, for instance, the governmental system was a means of facilitating efficient administration, while Awolowo regarded it as a philosophy of opportunity that would guarantee the autonomy of every ethnic group within the country, and also allow them to develop at their own desired pace (Awa 1964, p. 27). As shown above, both leaders and their northern counterparts were unanimous in their belief that federalism was the most suitable governmental system for accommodating the country's diversity. In other words, federalism was adopted to resolve the contradictions intrinsic to ethnocultural multiplicity. This provides an explanation for why the emergent federation recognised the cultural, ethnic, religious and other forms of diversity in the country.

The origin of the Nigerian federation may have thrown up divergent views but there is no disagreement over the fact that the country is a creation of British imperialism. The British colonialists brought together peoples of diverse ethnic, cultural, religious and linguistic backgrounds in one large political unit now known as Nigeria. These forces distinguish groups of people living in one concentrated area from those of other areas, explaining why they are crucial to our understanding of the operation of federalism in Nigeria. In what follows, therefore, we highlight the main forces within Nigeria's federal society. But what is a federal society?

Federal Society: What Does It Mean?

The term 'federal society' is usually construed in terms of the juxtaposition between 'social homogeneity', as exemplified by the federations of Australia, Austria and Germany, and 'social heterogeneity', as found in such federal states as Belgium, Canada, India, Malaysia, Nigeria and Switzerland (Burgess 2006, p. 140). But what does the term mean? The seed of the discussion over what constitutes federal society was sown by William S. Livingston in his article entitled 'A Note on the Nature of Federalism', first published in 1952. In that seminal article, which may be regarded as a critique of Wheare's notion of federalism, he argued that federal governments and federal constitutions do not 'grow simply and purely by accident'; they are consciously adopted to respond to certain societal stimuli, so 'federal government is a device by which the federal qualities of the society are articulated and protected' (Livingston 1952, p. 84). The point being made here is that social diversities produce federalism and as such, the system is a function not of constitutions but of societies. Linguistic diversities, territorial identities, religious differences and other social cleavages inherent in a particular society have political salience, as they are crucial to the formation of the federation, and subsequently to the stability of the federation. Thus, for Livingston, federalism transcends the purview of legalism and is concerned with many other problems associated with political organisations. It is about the management of the politics of difference that usually characterise federations, that is, the recognition of and respect for diversity rather than a constitutional design.

According to Livingston (1952, pp. 84–85), since every society is intimately integrated in accordance with its own peculiar historical, cultural, economic, political and other determinants and each is composed of elements that feel themselves to be different from the other elements, it, therefore, follows that a federal society is one in which diversities are grouped territorially, that is geographically. In other words, where diversities are grouped in some other way, that is, not grouped territorially, then the society is not federal, and its political system will not be federal in form. Other scholars that have accepted Livingston's definition of federal society include Ronald Watts and Michael Stein. Watts (1966, p. 95) defined a federal society as that segment of the spectrum (of societies) in which the 'pressures for unity and diversity are fairly closely balanced'. Thus, in a federal society, forces making for diversity are in approximate balance with forces making for unity. And for Stein (1968, p. 729):

> The concept of federal society can be most usefully applied if it is confined to a society that is both polyethnic and multilingual in makeup. The major cleavage defining societies of this type is a product of ethnic and linguistic differences. Where a society is constituted of territorially based communities that are clearly differentiated by language and ethnicity, then one can expect to find a federal society.

Clearly, the question of territoriality is important to the federal society discourse. For Livingston (1952, p. 86), federalism becomes nothing if the diversities are not territorially grouped. Livingston was not alone in focusing on territorial division of power, as Stein (1968, p. 725) also argued that where diversities are grouped territorially, the likelihood is that these territories will be assigned functions appropriate to their diversities, and federal forms will be established. Similarly, for Dikshit (1975, p. 10), federalism is the most geographically expressive of all forms of government because of the fact that it is based 'on the existence of regional differences or a sense of locality'. Central to this discourse is that federalism recognises the existence of territorially grouped diversities.

Territoriality is a significant factor when dealing with sociological variables, but should not be viewed in absolute terms because it incorporates an amalgam of other factors such as religion, geography and the economy to produce complex forms of political identity (Burgess 2006, p. 141). As the case of Nigeria demonstrates, in practice, territorial identity interacts with other social cleavages to produce distinct identities or distinctive communities. It is, however, important to point out that the idea that federalism is an ideal political framework for deeply divided countries, that is, countries with a high degree of social heterogeneity, has been dismissed as 'sociological fallacy' by scholars opposed to the idea. Brian Galligan, for instance, maintains that the governmental system is ultimately well suited not to the sort of social heterogeneity endemic in multinational issues, but rather to the relative social homogeneity characteristic of Australia (Galligan 1995, p. 55, quoted in Burgess 2006, p. 108). It must, however, be emphasised that this viewpoint does not exclude the option that federalism might be adopted in multi-ethnic societies like Nigeria.

As noted earlier, such diversities as differences of ethnicity, economic interest, religion, nationality, and variations in size and others combined to induce the Federation of Nigeria and as such must be given recognition. Therefore, from this, our definition of the concept of federal society includes those unifying and separating forces embedded in Nigerian society. These forces have high political salience, and to ignore them is to deny ourselves a proper analysis of federalism in a multinational federation such as Nigeria.

Ethnicity as Element of Nigeria's Federal Society

Mention has been made of the various colonial constitutional engineering embarked upon in the name of forging a sense of unity amongst the peoples that inhabit Nigeria but it has to be said that these efforts were simply a requisite of colonial administration. The adoption of a common administrative system and a lingua franca, for example, were intended to facilitate administrative efficiency, to make life easy for the colonial administrators and not to create a Nigerian nation. This view was vehemently reiterated by some of the country's founding fathers. For example, in 1947 the then Premier of the Western Region, Chief Obafemi Awolowo, wrote in his famous book *Path to Nigerian Freedom* that:

> Nigeria is not a nation. It is a mere geographical expression. There are no 'Nigerians' in the same sense as there are 'English', 'Welsh' or 'French'. The word 'Nigerian' is merely a distinctive appellation to distinguish those who live within the boundaries of Nigeria from those who do not. (Awolowo 1947, pp. 47–48)

Implicitly reacting to Awolowo's statement, in 1948 another leader, this time from the North, Sir Abubakar Tafawa Balewa, remarked in the Legislative Council that:

> Since 1914 the British Government has been trying to make Nigeria into one country, but the Nigerian people themselves are historically different in their backgrounds, in their religious beliefs and customs and do not show themselves any sign of willingness to unite. ... Nigerian unity is only a British intention for the country. (*Legislative Council Debate*, Nigeria, March 4, 1948, p. 227, quoted in Coleman 1958, p. 320)

These late statesmen were right in their assertions that Britain's plan for the former colony, as in the rest of the dependencies, did not include the building of a nation. The British had not come to West Africa on a mission of nation building, but simply to trade. Bringing different peoples under one gigantic territorial umbrella was to later lay the foundation for the assertion of all sorts of identity and loyalty among the different nations in the country. Despite the amalgamation that tended to bring the peoples of Nigeria together and the efforts made by the colonialists, citizens still preferred to identify with sub-national or ethnic groups for protection against 'others'. In their attempts to forge unity, the country's founding fathers deliberately chose as the national motto 'Unity and Faith', and also included the line in the national anthem: 'Though tribe and tongue may differ, in brotherhood we stand' (Kirk-Greene 1967, pp. 3–4). In reality, however, Nigeria's political leaders tend to promote a cleavage structure for their own selfish interests, and this may be an explanation for their inability to foster an agenda capable of bringing about any sense of national identity. It is not unusual for leaders to rally their kinsmen and kinswomen to promote their political aspirations. Unsurprisingly, the politicisation of ethnicity remains an integral part of Nigeria's federal society.

Politics in Nigeria is often characterised by the divisive struggle among ethnic, and sometimes, regional groups over control of national resources. Ethnicity plays an important part in determining who gets what and when. Inter-ethnic competition more often than not provokes tension, explaining why ethnic conflicts have become almost inevitable in the country. The inequality among the ethnic groups gives rise to the politics of suspicion, fear of domination and zero-sum competition for the country's resources. As a result, the social, political and economic import of ethnicity cannot be ignored if an insightful analysis of Nigerian politics is to be undertaken. Although reducing the interplay of contending forces in the politics of the multi-ethnic federation solely to ethnicity would be tantamount to a one-dimensional argument, this social phenomenon cannot be ignored; it remains a considerable factor in the distribution of the country's resources.

Religion as Element of Nigeria's Federal Society

Religion is a social cleavage that should be viewed as part of a larger cultural identity. It is also of political significance. As argued by Burgess (2006, p. 142), religion is a cultural–ideological cleavage that is difficult to engage for the purpose of negotiation because it is a non-bargainable issue entailing metaphysical issues about faith and the human spirit that are non-negotiable. Religious differences have high political salience in federations such as India, Malaysia and Nigeria. In Nigeria, religion interacts with regionalism and territoriality in the same manner that regionalism and ethnic identity reinforce each other. Nigeria is not only multi-ethnic; it is also multi-religious. One significant feature of Nigeria as a multi-religious federation is the cross-cutting nature of the religious cleavage. Hence, religious differences must be treated as part of the larger constellation of cleavage patterns in the country.

When it comes to the issue of religion, non-Nigerian commentators, more often than not, divide the country along the so-called 'Muslim north and Christian south', a division that has continued to exacerbate the north-south dichotomy. It is not unusual for some to say that Nigeria's population is evenly divided between Christians and Muslims. There is no denying that Christianity and Islam form the two dominant religions in Nigeria, but putting the population in the aforementioned categories amounts to oversimplifying the country's complex religious identity. There exists a tiny minority who practise 'indigenous/traditional' religions and those who practise none. Traditional religious practices continue to flourish in every part of the country. Besides, the concept of 'Muslim-north' may be misleading as the northern part of the country is inhabited by Christians as well, especially in the middle-belt. The same applies to that of 'Christian-south'.

In Nigeria, religious identity overlaps not only with ethnic identity but also with regional identity, and it is not difficult to see how ethno-regional and religious identities conjoin. For example, the north-west geopolitical region of the country is populated mainly by the Hausa-Fulani Muslims, while the majority of inhabitants in the north-east are also Muslims. However, north-central Nigeria is culturally and religiously mixed. The south-west, inhabited mainly by the Yoruba, is also religiously mixed but culturally homogenous. Many extended families in this region are a mixture of both, providing an explanation for the rarity of inter-confessional conflicts (Babalola 2018, p. 40). In the south-east are the Igbo, who are predominantly Christian, and the south-south, also referred to as the Niger Delta region, is home to minority ethnic groups who are just as clearly Christians.

Islam came to northern Nigeria some thousand years ago. The Jihad of Uthman Dan Fodio of the nineteenth century which overthrew the corrupt and repressive administration of the *Sarakunas* (Hausa kings) established the Sokoto Caliphate, 'a federation of emirates', thereby facilitating the spread of the religion across the northern region (Ibrahim 1991; Kenny 1996; Onapajo 2012). In keeping with the promise made by Lord Lugard to the northern traditional rulers that the British government would not interfere with their religion, the colonialists ensured that Christian proselytisation was not allowed in the emirates (Kenny 1996, p. 340). It may be argued that the British prevented the northerners from interacting with Christian Missionaries, mostly based in the south, so that they would not have the opportunity to acquire Western education, which had the capacity to instil in them some form of political consciousness which might, in turn, put them on a collision course with the traditional institutions that had contributed to the immense success of the indirect rule policy in the region. As aptly observed by Kirk-Greene (1967, p. 5), Christianity fought an uphill battle against the stronger social appeal of Islam in the then Northern Nigeria, and this partly explains why today, about 75% of the population in the North are Muslims. Colonialism succeeded in implanting Christianity in southern Nigeria, whilst it prevented its spread in the north. The commercial relationship that existed between the Yoruba-speaking people and the peoples of the north, particularly the Nupe and Fulani, helped in the spread of Islam in the Yoruba traditional societies (Onapajo 2012, p. 45).

Christianity, on the other hand, was first introduced into the coastal areas of the Niger Delta region by Christian Missionaries in the fifteenth century and then to the rest of southern Nigeria (Onapajo 2012, p. 45). The spread of Christianity was believed to be boosted by the religion's disdain for the slave trade, and its promotion of Western education. The religion also sought to eradicate certain traditional practices associated with traditional African religions such as human sacrifices, the killing of twins and other practices considered barbaric and uncivilised. Nonetheless, the religion did not have a smooth ride in the north, partly because Islam had already taken root there. As mentioned earlier, another reason for this was the deliberate colonial policy that ensured non-interference with traditional institutions, including Islam, in northern Nigeria.

The impact of religion on the politics of Nigeria cannot be ignored. Religious diversity has continued to constitute a strong divisive source of conflict.

Conclusion

In this chapter, we have demonstrated that the British colonialists did not impose federalism on Nigeria. There is no denying that they promoted the federal idea but the founding fathers' desire to have a federal union cannot be ignored in the analysis of the emergence of the federation. Just like the colonialists, the nationalists favoured the idea with the belief that the differences among the Nigerian peoples in terms of language, religion and historical background could only be accommodated in a federation. The presence of such prerequisites as the hope of economic advantage, geographical contiguity, ethno-cultural variation, some previous political association, and similarity of political institutions are particularly instructive to the formation of the federation. The historical impact of British rule on the formation of the federation is apparent, but to reject the social and economic conditions that laid the foundation for the federal state is to make light of the importance of the forces that combined to result in the transformation of the previously unitary state into a federation. It makes sense to describe Nigeria as a British creation, but to argue that its federal system was imposed on the peoples of the territories that later formed themselves into a federal union may be a misinterpretation of Nigeria's political history. Imposed federations should be sought in the new federal models exemplified by Bosnia and Herzegovina, and Iraq. It may be concluded that in Nigeria, the British colonial government promoted the federal idea as it had done in India, initially for administrative convenience, and later as a means of managing the country's multiple diversities.

The chapter has also depicted a picture of a country characterised mainly by ethno-linguistic and religious divisions. Given these centrifugal tendencies, therefore, one may argue that creating the Nigerian state seemed easier than creating a Nigerian nation. The colonial system of divide-and-rule pitched one ethnic group against the other, thereby reinforcing ethnic differences and sentiments. The system of administration promoted bitterness and resentment among the different ethnic groups. It is, therefore, not out of place to argue that the British implicitly promoted sub-nationalism rather than national identity in the country. It is also a plausible argument that Nigeria's present problems are partly rooted in its multiplicity. Indeed, diversities within Nigeria's federal society have thrown up so many religious, cultural, economic and all sorts of other questions that it has become difficult to lay a finger on what constitutes the national question in Nigeria today. Without a doubt, the diversity inherent in the country's federal society made the choice of a federal system obtainable, but this also made the development of common attitude difficult.

As already argued, federalism was promoted in Nigeria with the belief that the system has the ability to promote unity in diversity. Any reform must, therefore, ensure the accommodation of the country's ethnic diversity because this is one of the many ways national unity could be achieved.

References

Afigbo, A. (1991). Background to Nigerian Federalism: Federal Features in the Colonial State. *Publius: The Journal of Federalism, 21*(4), 13–29.

Awa, E. (1964). *Federal Government in Nigeria*. Berkeley and Los Angeles: University of California Press.

Awa, E. (1976). *Issues in Federalism*. Benin City: Ethiope Publishing Corporation.

Awolowo, O. (1947). *Path to Nigerian Freedom*. London: Faber and Faber.

Ayoade, J. A. A. (1973). Secession Threat as a Redressive Mechanism in Nigerian Federalism. *Publius: The Journal of Federalism, 3*, 57–75.

Babalola, D. (2018). Ethnicity, Ethnic Conflict and the Elusive Quest for Peace in Post-military Nigeria. In D. Babalola & H. Onapajo (Eds.), *Nigeria, a Country Under Siege: Issues of Conflict and Its Management*. Newcastle upon Tyne: Cambridge Scholars Publishing.

Balewa, T. (1964). *Mr Prime Minister*. Lagos: Government Printer.

Ballard, J. (1971, October). Administrative Origins of Nigerian Federalism. *African Affairs, 70*(281), 333–348.

Bello, A. (1962). *My Life: An Autobiography*. Cambridge: University Press.

Birch, A. (1966). Approaches to the Study of Federalism. *Political Studies, 14*, 15–33.

Burgess, M. (1999). Obstinate or Obsolete? The State of the Canadian Federation. *Regional & Federal Studies, 9*(2), 1–15.

Burgess, M. (2006). *Comparative Federalism: Theory and Practice*. London and New York: Routledge.

Burgess, M. (2012). *In Search of the Federal Spirit: New Theoretical and Empirical Perspectives in Comparative Federalism*. Oxford: Oxford University Press.

Coleman, J. (1958). *Nigeria: Background to Nationalism*. Los Angeles: University of California Press.

Davis, R. (1978). *The Federal Principle: A Journey Through Time in Quest of Meaning*. Berkeley, Los Angeles, and London: University of California Press.

Dikshit, R. (1975). *The Political Geography of Federalism: An Enquiry into Origins and Stability*. New Delhi: Macmillan.

Elaigwu, J. (2007). *The Politics of Federalism in Nigeria*. London: Adonis & Abbey Publishers.

Eleazu, U. (1977). *Federalism and Nation Building: The Nigerian Experience 1954–1964*. Devon: Arthur H. Stockwell.

Galligan, B. (1995). *A Federal Republic: Australia's Constitutional System of Government*. Cambridge: Cambridge University Press.

Habtu, A. (2005). Multiethnic Federalism in Ethiopia: A Study of the Secession Clause in the Constitution. *Publius: Journal of Federalism, 35*(2), 313–335.

Hicks, U. (1978). *Federalism: Failure and Success—A Comparative Study*. London and Basingstoke: Macmillan.

Ibrahim, J. (1991). Religion and Political Turbulence in Nigeria. *Journal of Modern African Studies, 29*(1), 115–136.

Keil, S. (2013). *Multinational Federalism in Bosnia and Herzegovina*. Surrey: Ashgate.

Keller, E. (2002). Ethnic Federalism, Fiscal Reform, Development and Democracy in Ethiopia. *African Journal of Political Science, 7*(1), 21–50.

Kenny, J. (1996). Sharia and Christianity in Nigeria: Islam and a 'Secular State'. *Journal of Religion in Africa, 26*(4), 338–364.
King, P. (1982). *Federalism and Federation*. Baltimore: Johns Hopkins University Press.
Kirk-Greene, A. H. M. (1967). The Peoples of Nigeria: The Cultural Background to the Crisis. *African Affairs, 262*, 3–11.
Livingston, W. (1952). A Note on the Nature of Federalism. *Political Science Quarterly, 67*(1), 81–95.
Maddox, W. (1941, December). The Political Basis of Federation. *The American Political Science Review, 35*(6), 1120–1127.
McKay, D. (2004). William Riker on Federalism: Sometimes Wrong But More Right Than Anyone Else? *Regional & Federal Studies, 14*(2), 167–186.
Onapajo, H. (2012). Politics for God: Religion, Politics and Conflict in Democratic Nigeria. *The Journal of Pan African Studies, 4*(9), 42–66.
Osadolor, O. (1998). The Development of the Federal Idea and the Federal Framework, 1914–1960. In K. Amuwo, et al. (Eds.), *Federalism and Political Restructuring in Nigeria*. Ibadan: Spectrum Books Limited and IFRA.
Osuntokun, J. (1979). The Historical Background of Nigerian Federalism. In A. B. Akinyemi, et al. (Eds.), *Readings on Federalism* (pp. 91–102). Lagos, Nigeria: The Nigerian Institute of International Affairs (NIIA).
Oyovbaire, S. (1983). Structural Change and Political Processes in Nigeria. *African Affairs, 82*(326), 3–28.
Oyovbaire, S. (1985). *Federalism in Nigeria: A Study in the Development of the Nigerian State*. London: Macmillan.
Riker, W. (1964). *Federalism: Origin, Operation, Significance*. Boston: Little, Brown.
Shakir, F. (2017). *The Iraqi Federation: Origin, Operation and Significance*. London and New York: Routledge.
Stein, M. (1968). Federal Political Systems and Federal Societies. *World Politics, 20*(4), 721–747.
Stepan, A. (1999). Federalism and Democracy: Beyond the US Model. *Journal of Democracy, 10*(4), 19–34.
Stepan, A. (2001). *Arguing Comparative Politics*. Oxford: Oxford University Press.
Suberu, R. (2001). *Federalism and Ethnic Conflict in Nigeria*. Washington, DC: United States Institute of Peace Press.
Suberu, R. (2004). Nigeria: Dilemmas of Federalism. In U. M. Amoretti & N. Bermeo (Eds.), *Federalism and Territorial Cleavages*. Baltimore and London: Johns Hopkins University Press.
Watts, R. (1966). *New Federations: Experiments in the Commonwealth*. Oxford: Clarendon Press.

Wheare, K. (1962). Federalism and the Making of Nations. In A. W. Macmahon (Ed.), *Federalism: Mature and Emergent*. New York: Russell & Russell.
Wheare, K. (1963). *Federal Government* (4th ed.). London: Oxford University Press.
Woelk, J. (2004). Federalism and Consociationalism as Tools for State Reconstruction? The Case of Bosnia and Herzegovina. In G. A. Tarr, R. F. Williams, & J. Marka (Eds.), *Federalism, Subnational Constitutions, and Minority Rights*. Westport, CT, and London: Praeger.

CHAPTER 3

Oil Centrism and Nigeria's Political Economy

Introduction

Since this study is about how Nigeria's political economy shapes the country's federal system it, therefore, becomes imperative to examine the character of the political economy in detail. An examination of the political economy of Nigeria deserves to be taken seriously if any meaningful analysis of the federal system is to be undertaken. This is what this chapter aims to achieve. In doing so, we examine the salient feature of the political economy, namely, oil dependency. The Nigerian state operates an oil-centred economy, with all other sectors, as well as governments at all levels dependent upon the oil sector. The centrality of oil to the political economy of the country and the intrinsic relationship between this natural resource and the Nigerian state cannot be overemphasised. In what follows, the political economy of Nigeria is examined within the context of the rentier political economy approach, which principally dwells on the consequences of over-dependency on oil. Nigeria's oil wealth has not provided the needed stimulus for growth, nor has it spurred political stability. This is a paradox. In Nigeria, oil revenue does not provide the impetus for growth in other sectors of the economy. The question, therefore, is why has the country's economic record, despite the oil wealth, been characterised by a lack of growth, increasing poverty and systemic corruption? What are the effects of Nigeria's mono-product economy on politics?

D. Babalola, *The Political Economy of Federalism in Nigeria*, Federalism and Internal Conflicts,
https://doi.org/10.1007/978-3-030-05493-9_3

The remainder of the chapter is organised into three main sections. In the first section, we trace the integration of the Nigerian economy into the global economic system. An understanding of the historical context of Nigeria's political economy is necessary for a full understanding of its current state. The second section adopts the rentier thesis to examine the underlying features of Nigeria's political economy such as oil-dependency and corruption. In this section, attempts are made to highlight the inherent contradictions in Nigeria's oil-centric economy. Put simply, the section is about the effects of the country's oil-dependency upon the country's politics. The final section concludes the chapter.

The Integration of the Nigerian Economy into the Global Economic System

Nigeria and other African countries became actors on the world economic stage when legitimate trade replaced the slave trade (Aboyade 1966). This period coincided with the advent of the Industrial Revolution of the nineteenth century, which gave rise to an increased demand for tropical raw materials by European industries. The hitherto trading relationship between Europe and Africa characterised by the slave trade had to be jettisoned for a new relationship. The ensued relationship meant that Africa was to supply Europe with raw materials and Europe was to supply Africa with manufactured goods. The need for the post-Second World War reconstruction in Europe particularly resulted in increased demand for Nigerian agricultural products. This marked the beginning of the period Nigeria became a source of raw materials such as cotton, cocoa, rubber, palm produce and timber for British industries.

In order to further British economic interest in Nigeria, the former had to, first and foremost, integrate the latter's economy into the global capitalist economic system. One of the steps taken by the colonial authorities, therefore, to ensure effective integration was to monetise the economy. According to Ake (1981, p. 33), monetisation of an economy means the presence of money as a means of exchange, and the development of the modern monetary system including the credit system. Monetisation ensured the introduction of a universally accepted medium of exchange, which could be used for the importation of European manufactured goods. In pre-colonial Nigeria, the main medium of exchange was barter where commodities were directly exchanged for other commodities. This method of conducting trade lacked a common unit of exchange. Due to this limitation, therefore, the method was replaced with commodity currencies such as cases or bottles of local gin, brass pans, cowries, shells and small alloy horseshoes called 'manila' (Ake 1981, p. 32; Coleman 1958, pp. 56–57). The commodity currencies too had their limitations; they were not convertible into international currencies.

As part of its monetisation efforts, the British established the West African Currency Board in 1912 to issue a separate currency for its colonies in West Africa. Britain ensured that both the British and the West African currencies were convertible. This effectively tied the African colonial economies to that of the 'mother country' (metropole). In other words, the Nigerian colonial economy became an extension of the British economy. Moreover, since the money supply was determined mainly by the demand for the colonies' exports, it meant that the colonial economies depended upon the British economy. According to Rodney (1972, p. 34), African economies, in general, were integrated into the world capitalist economies in a manner that ensured that Africa was dependent on the big capitalist countries.

African economies were also monetised by imposing taxes on the African people. These taxes had to be paid with the European currency. Nigerians, in particular, were not new to paying taxes but they were new to paying taxes with the European currency. Compulsory payment of taxes in this new fashion, therefore, forced every household, either to turn to wage labour, especially in the railways and coal mines or to produce cash crops that could be sold for money, through which tax could be paid. As posited by Coleman (1958, p. 57), systematic taxation was one of the most effective colonial government measures in the development of a money economy in Nigeria. Likewise, the demand and supply of agricultural products gave rise to the development of a money market, as part of the income generated by the people of the colony from colonial trade went into the consumption of imported manufactured goods as well as payment of tax. Monetising the colonial economy did not only facilitate the integration of the Nigerian economy into the world capitalist system; it also brought about guaranteed revenue for the colonial government. However, it should be noted that the colony's ability to purchase manufactured goods depended on its export of primary products. The obvious consequence was the structural dependence of the Nigerian economy on the British economy.

The need for the colonies to produce raw materials needed in Europe, which was to produce manufactured goods consumed in the colonies resulted in a process of international exchange between the African economies and those of Europe. Of significance is that the terms under which this 'specialisation' took place were lopsided in favour of Europe. The production and sale of these commodities were undertaken under the terms dictated by the metropole. In the case of Nigeria, for instance, the British determined the demand for and the supply of goods, as well as the qualities of the goods exported to Britain whereas, Nigeria did not have a say in what was produced in Britain and imported into Nigeria.

The economic relations between Africa and Europe were characterised by what Samir Amin referred to as 'unequal exchange' (Amin 1981, p. 37). For a better understanding of the political economy of Africa in general, Amin divided the continent into three broad macro-regions, namely, 'Africa of the colonial trade economy' which consists of Ghana, Nigeria, Sierra Leone, Gambia, Liberia, Guinea-Bissau, Togo, Cameroun, Chad and the Sudan; 'Africa of the labour reserves', consisting of countries in the eastern and southern parts of Africa, including Kenya, Uganda, Tanzania, Rwanda, Burundi, Malawi, Angola, Mozambique, Zimbabwe, Botswana, Lesotho, Swaziland and South Africa; and 'Africa of the concession-owning companies'. This last category consists of countries in the traditional Congo River Basin and they include Congo-Kinshasa, Congo-Brazzaville, Gabon and the Central African Republic. This categorisation was based on the resources that could be exploited by the colonial powers in these regions. According to Amin (1981), the economic development of 'Africa of the labour reserves' region was conditioned by the need for large amounts of labour for the mines found in that region, whereas the territories in the 'Africa of the concession-owning companies' were given to concessionary companies, whose main objective was to exploit the territories while providing a minimum of investment, and the 'Africa of the colonial trade economy' was thus characterised by a subordination/domination relationship between Africa and Europe (pp. 28–40). The unequal exchange that characterised colonial trade, particularly between Britain and its colonies, Nigeria included, sustained the British economy in the period immediately following the Second World War. Of course, it is not difficult to see the dialectical relationship between development and underdevelopment, particularly how one helps to produce the other. Rodney (1972, p. 85) puts this more succinctly, arguing that, 'Africa helped to develop Western Europe in the same proportion as Western Europe helped to underdevelop Africa'.

Also important in the integration process is the role played by the colonial state in protecting mercantile companies such as the British-controlled United Africa Company (UAC) in the colonial economy. The UAC controlled Nigeria's export-import trade and thus played a dominant role in the Nigerian economy. As a result of the support and protection from the colonial state, foreign traders were able to out-compete their African counterparts, some of whom had no choice but to become wage earners or middlemen for European firms. The colonial state guaranteed conducive business atmosphere under which private foreign companies could operate in Africa.

Moreover, the introduction of the produce marketing boards in Nigeria also facilitated the integration process. Colonial Nigeria's four main export crops (cocoa, palm produce, groundnut, and cotton) were collected and marketed through the Nigerian Cocoa Marketing Board (1947), the Nigerian Palm Produce Marketing Board (1949), the Nigerian Groundnut Produce Marketing Board (1949) and the Nigerian Cotton Marketing Board (1949) respectively (Ake 1981, p. 64). These boards assumed a monopsony status because they were the only purchasers of agricultural products. The colonial state ensured that the boards had no competitors. There is no denying that the boards became sources of revenue for the colonial government but they also became agencies of exploitation. For example, the boards usually purchased goods from the peasant farmers at figures that were below world market prices.[1]

Trade also contributed to the integration process. Since the expansion of trade required infrastructural development, the colonial government had to construct roads and railroads, for example. Of course, these infrastructures were utilised within the colonies but they implicitly linked the colonies with Europe. This is because they facilitated the transportation of bulk agricultural products from the producing areas to the ports, where they were exported to the metropolitan countries. This explains why the dependency theorists usually argue that the infrastructures provided in the colonies were meant to serve the interests of the colonialists.

[1]According to Rodney (1972, p. 185), the West African Produce Board paid Nigerians £16.15s for a ton of palm oil in 1946 and sold that through the Ministry of Food for £95, which was nearer to the world market price. Groundnuts were bought for £15 per ton by the Boards and later sold in Britain at £110 per ton.

So, the supposed benefits of colonialism were circumstantial and not intended to benefit the colonial states.

As capitalism became firmly rooted in colonial Nigeria, the economy became more compatible with the British economy. With the transformation of the economic system, socio-economic life also became transformed. Nigerians now had to earn cash either to pay tax or to purchase imported manufactured goods. Nigerian farmers, traders and wage earners, especially those in the agricultural sector became dependent for their livelihood on the market for export crops. Also, because the economy was dominated by foreign trade, foreign exchange earnings were dependent upon the vagaries of the global market for primary commodities.

The Pre-oil Political Economy

It is clear from the foregoing section that agriculture dominated the colonial economy. Crude oil was discovered in Nigeria in commercial quantity in 1956 but the oil boom of the early 1970s facilitated the transformation of the previously agriculture-driven economy to an oil-centred economy. Earnings from agricultural exports contributed, in no small measure, to Nigeria's economic growth until the 1960s. It is on record that before the discovery of oil, the country was the world's largest exporter of groundnuts and palm produce and the second largest exporter of cocoa. These three crops provided about 70% of the value of Nigerian exports (Kirk-Greene and Rimmer 1981, p. 74). According to Graf (1988, p. 30), the total regional revenues in 1961 comprised 58.55% from the Western Region, 25.7% from the Eastern Region, and 15.7% from the Northern Region and the percentages of the national aggregate of personal taxes collected from the regions in the same year were 67.7% (Western Region), 27.2% (Eastern Region), and 9% (Northern Region). The table shows the contribution of agriculture to the country's national revenue between 1954 and 1961 (Table 3.1).

It is evident from the table that the regionalisation of the marketing boards that took place in 1954 when the federal system was adopted allowed the regional governments to garner enormous revenue, part of which went into regional development programmes. For example, the Northern Region was rich in the production of cotton and groundnuts, while the Eastern Region was also rich in palm produce, and the Western Region was the richest due to cocoa production. Although it could be argued that the disparity in agricultural production accentuated the

Table 3.1 Total accumulation by Nigerian Marketing Boards 1954–1961 (£'000)

Item	*Eastern Region*	*Northern Region*	*Western Region*	*Total*
Transfer from commodity board	11,464.1	32,651.8	42,897.2	87,013.1
Net trading surplus	10,736.2	3202.7	14,303.9	21,837.1
Excess of income over expenditure	1718.9	2451.2	5349.1	9519.2
Total	23,919.2	38,305.7	62,550.2	118,369.4

Source Bangura et al. (1986, p. 176)

unequal development that characterised the constituent units during the First Republic (1960–1966), agricultural contribution to the country's national revenue cannot be overemphasised. Moreover, the fiscal autonomy enjoyed by the constituent units also resulted in the expansion of regional powers and the weakening of the federal centre.

Regional political/business elites, taking advantage of their easy access to credit facilities, turned the marketing boards into conduits for private capital accumulation. The riches so acquired provided them with an enabling environment to transform themselves into commercial capitalists,[2] serving as middlemen for the mercantile firms who bought agricultural goods from Nigerian peasant farmers, and sold manufactured goods to farmers and wage earners within what Aboyade (1966) has referred to as a 'trading economy'. Moreover, their wealth put them in a position where they determined who gets what in the Regions. Consequently, the Regions became political battlefields for regional elites and political parties. In Nigeria, access to the state means access to state resources, which in turn means the economic advancement of the individual and sometimes of the individual's ethnic group. Political power is synonymous with economic power and it is a weapon to access some share of the

[2] Indigenous businesspeople are referred to as commercial capitalists because they lack a productive base of their own in any real economic sense, only profiting from produce buying and selling. For more on the activities of this class in relation to the Nigerian economy, see Turner, T. (1978), 'Commercial Capitalism and the 1975 Coup', in Panter-Brick, S. K. (ed.), *Soldiers and Oil: The Political Transformation of Nigeria*, London: Frank Cass; and Williams, G. (1976), 'Nigeria: A Political Economy', in Williams, G. (ed.), *Nigeria: Economy and Society*, London: Rex Collings.

national resources. Nigerian politicians are known for taking advantage of their access to the office of the state to acquire wealth for themselves. This explains why most businessmen are in politics just as most politicians are in business. Politics is the most lucrative venture in the country. In Nigeria, political elites compete for some share of the 'national cake', which they then distribute to their own array of followers.

Nigeria as a Rentier State

Once we accept that oil is central to the political economy of Nigeria, it logically follows that the 'rentier' theory would be more apposite to study the political economy of the country. The approach primarily dwells on the consequences of a state's over-dependence on oil. It focuses on the state as the recipient and distributor of rent income and also explains how oil rents in particular impact on the nature of the states, as well as their political and economic systems. The 'rentier' thesis was postulated by Hossein Mahdavy in 1970 to analyse the impacts of oil rents on the politics and economy of pre-revolutionary Pahlavi Iran (Mahdavy 1970). The theory has since been adopted by a group of scholars to analyse the politics and economies of resource-dependent states such as Libya (First 1980), Gabon (Yates 1996), and Venezuela (Karl 1997). What scholars of the rentier persuasion do is to focus on the effects of oil rents on a given state and its corresponding economy.

Let us begin by defining the concept of 'rent'. To classical economists, a rent meant a payment for use of land or an income for a landlord. In its contemporary usage, rent means an income for landlords, as well as a 'reward for ownership of all natural resources' (Beblawi 1987, p. 49).[3] Likewise, Collier (2008) also defined rent as the excess of revenues overall costs generated by natural resources. Following on from these definitions, therefore, we define rent as royalties paid on natural resources. Who then is a rentier? According to Beblawi (1987, p. 50), a rentier is a member of a social group, who 'does not participate actively in the economic production, receives nevertheless a share in the produce and at

[3] Beblawi, H. (1987), 'The Rentier State in the Arab World', in Beblawi, H. and Luciani, G. (eds.), *The Rentier State*, London: Croom Helm. This work has been re-published in *Arab Studies Quarterly*, Vol. 9, No. 4 (Fall 1987), pp. 383–398; and in Luciani, G. (ed.) (1990), *The Arab State*, Berkeley and Los Angeles: University of California Press, pp. 85–98. For convenience, therefore, we have chosen to cite the earliest version.

times a handsome share'. Thus, a rentier may be defined as that individual or state that lives on income from natural resources.

Rentier states, according to Mahdavy (1970, p. 428), are 'those countries that receive on a regular basis, substantial amounts of external rent', and external rents are 'rentals paid by foreign individuals, concerns or governments to individuals, concerns or governments of a given country'. This definition implies that oil revenue generated by governments of oil-exporting states is external rent, and the receiving state is a rentier state. Mahdavy's definition has generally been accepted. However, Beblawi and Luciani have rejected its underlying meaning on the ground that it focuses excessively on the state rather than the economy. For them, focusing exclusively on the state, independently of the economy, and defining as rentier any state that derives a substantial part of its revenue from foreign sources and in the form of economic rent, is 'a rather restrictive definition that says little about the economy' as the rentier state is 'a subsystem associated with a rentier economy' (Beblawi and Luciani 1987, p. 11). These scholars prefer to put greater emphasis on the economy, and as such define a 'rentier economy' as one in which rent plays a major role, and in which that rent comes from external sources.

Beblawi concurred with Mahdavy's view that the stage at which a country assumes a rentier status is determined arbitrarily, and the determination of when an economy becomes rentier is a matter of judgment. However, Beblawi (1987, p. 52) identified four characteristics which a state must possess for it to be referred to as a *rentier*. First, a rentier economy should be characterised as one in which 'rent situations predominate'. Second, a rentier economy must be one that relies on substantial external rent. Thus, the rent must come from foreign sources. The presence of domestic rents, even if they were substantial, 'is not sufficient to characterise a rentier economy'. Third, in a rentier state, 'only a few are engaged in the generation of rent (wealth)', while the majority are only involved in the distribution and utilisation (consumption) of the wealth generated. Fourth, in a rentier state, the government is 'the principal recipient of the external rent in the economy'. Thus, external rents are received without much economic input from the domestic economy of the receiving country. Moreover, rentier states are substantially financed through externally generated revenues rather than through internally generated revenues.

Agreeing with Mahdavy and Beblawi, Luciani (1987, p. 69) posits that oil exports have the tendency to 'free the state from the need of raising income domestically'.[4] Luciani takes this freedom that rent provides to the state from the need to extract income internally as a point of departure, and categorises states as 'Allocation' and 'Production' states. While the 'production state' relies on the domestic economy for its income, an 'allocation state' does not depend on domestic sources of revenue and is only sustained by the economy of the oil importing countries. For Luciani, therefore, rentier states are allocation states, 'whose revenue derives predominantly (more than 40%) from oil or other foreign sources and whose expenditure is a substantial share of GDP' (p. 70). Given the foregoing definitions, Nigeria, no doubt, perfectly typifies a rentier state, and its economy, a rentier economy because oil rent constitutes a substantial part of its foreign exchange earnings. Recent research shows that oil accounts for about 95% of the country's total foreign exchange earnings, and generates over 40% of the country's Gross Domestic Product (GDP) (Ejobowah 2010, p. 265; ICG 2006, p. 19; White and Taylor 2001, p. 333). Oil plays a pivotal role in the political economy of Nigeria. This is not suggesting that the oil-rich country does not have other sources of revenue like corporate tax, value-added tax (VAT) and personal income tax, but oil revenue constitutes its dominant source of wealth. Nigeria's political and economic fate is, evidently tied to oil-generated wealth. This reliance effectively goes back to the early 1970s, when oil-exporting countries including Nigeria witnessed a boom in oil revenue. Since the boom period, budgets are usually predicated upon the projected annual production as well as the price in the international oil market. The massive oil revenue enjoyed by the Nigerian state and other rentier states during the period was as a result of pressure from the Organisation of Petroleum Exporting Countries (OPEC), which quadrupled oil prices.

Oil Rents and the Nigerian Political Economy

The advent of oil, no doubt, brought about a decline in the contribution of agriculture to national revenue. According to statistics, Nigeria's agricultural products in 1962 accounted for about 70% of the total

[4]Luciani, G. (1987), 'Allocation vs. Production States', in Beblawi, H. and Luciani, G. (eds.), *The Rentier State*, London: Croom Helm, p. 69; This work has been re-published in G. Luciani (ed.) (1990), *The Arab State*, Berkeley and Los Angeles: University of California Press. However, we have chosen to cite the earlier version.

export value, but by 1974, agriculture's share of total export earnings had dropped to less than 20%, whereas petroleum's share of the total earnings accounted for only 10% of export earnings in 1962, but rose to 82.7% in 1973 (Bangura et al. 1986, p. 177). Similarly, as observed by Khan (1994, p. 187), between 1970 and 1982, yearly production of the main Nigerian cash crops, such as cocoa, rubber, cotton and groundnuts, fell by 43, 29, 65 and 64% respectively.

What these statistics show is that the unprecedented flow of oil rents into the national revenue had caused the country's agricultural export goods to become unprofitable. Another reason for the decline in agricultural production is that the emergent oil sector witnessed a surge of capital and labour because the returns are higher than in agriculture. Consequently, Nigeria, a previously food exporter became a major food importer in the international food market.

There is little doubt that the massive inflow of oil rents into the Nigerian economy has afflicted Nigeria with the economic 'ailment' commonly known as the 'Dutch Disease'. The Dutch Disease is an economic problem used to describe the economic woes caused by over-dependence on a particular export commodity such as oil. The term was first used in the 1970s to explain the effect of North Sea gas on the economy of the Netherlands.[5] During this period, the Dutch economy experienced a surge in external rents, and this, in turn, caused capital and labour to be reallocated from previously productive sectors such as agriculture and manufacturing to the booming sector (Brass 2008, p. 527; Collier 2008, p. 39; Khan 1994, p. 183; Ross 1999, pp. 305–306; Yates 1996, pp. 27–28). In a similar fashion, the expansion of Nigeria's oil industry, which began in the early 1970s, brought about a neglect of the agricultural sector, which was the bedrock of the economy, a classic syndrome of the 'Dutch Disease'.

One major problem often linked to a rentier economy is that since the economy thrives on external rents, domestic production becomes insignificant. As argued by Mahdavy (1970, p. 429), 'however one looks at them, the oil revenues received by the governments of the oil exporting countries have very little to do with the production processes of their domestic economies … the inputs from the local economies …

[5]According to Michael Ross, the name was reputedly coined by *The Economist* in 1977 to refer to all economic hardships associated with resource exports. See Ross, M. (1999), 'The Political Economy of the Resource Curse', *World Politics* 51 (January), pp. 279–322.

are insignificant'. If well interpreted, the argument here is that there is no economic linkage between oil production and the domestic economies of rentier states. Ideally, the injection of funds into an economy is expected to lead to an increase in national income, which in turn gives rise to domestic demand and supply. However, the opposite is the case in an oil-rentier economy, where oil rents are not ploughed back into productive economic activities. This has been the case in Nigeria where oil-generated revenue is spent mostly on foreign goods, consequently constituting a leakage from the economy. Another explanation usually offered by the rentier scholars for this lack of linkage-effect is that resources are often extracted by foreign investors, who repatriate their profits to their home countries rather than invest in the economy where the profits were made. In Nigeria, oil revenue does not provide the impetus for growth in other sectors of the economy.

It is evident that revenue from oil has brought significant expansion to the Nigerian economy but typical of a rentier economy, only the tertiary sector benefits from the boom while the primary and secondary sectors decline. The constant inflow of oil rents into the economy not only caused the neglect of agriculture but also led to the collapse of the manufacturing sector, which also becomes economically less profitable. As argued by Ruth First (1980, p. 120), in a rentier economy, 'the usual development process is reversed – instead of the progression from agriculture to industry to services; oil provokes the growth of only the third sector (services)'. This assertion fits the Nigerian case where the tertiary sector, particularly banking continues to flourish, depicting a picture of a growing economy when in reality there is nothing to suggest any iota of meaningful growth. Oil rents into the economy of an oil rentier state do have the tendency to portray the state as economically buoyant. Clearly, oil rents are the major components of the gross national product (GNP) and a high GNP gives the impression of a healthy economy, whereas, in reality, the opposite is the case. Mahdavy (1970, p. 437) puts this more aptly, arguing that rentier states create 'an impression of prosperity and growth', whereas in reality, the mass of the population may remain in poverty. In Nigeria, despite the continuous inflow of oil rents into the economy the gap between the 'haves' and the 'have-nots' continue to widen. Majority of Nigerians live below the poverty line.

Another frequently cited problem usually associated with oil-rentier economies is their vulnerability to price fluctuations in the international oil market. The argument here is that since rentier states are dependent upon the inflow of international capital, fluctuations tend to have negative effects on domestic economies. A situation of this nature was witnessed in Nigeria when the oil boom of the 1970s gave rise to a corresponding increased spending, and the oil price crash of the 1980s resulted in economic hardship. The crash in crude oil price resulted in a corresponding decline in the country's foreign exchange earnings. This led to a grave fiscal predicament for the then civilian administration, which had to contend with increased worsening of the citizens' standard of living. Similarly, between 2015 and 2016, over two-thirds of the states in Nigeria found themselves on the verge of bankruptcy when they experienced a drop in federal allocations. This resulted, in part, from the decline in oil-generated revenue, which was a consequence of the fall in the price of oil in the global oil market. The affected states struggled to pay workers' salaries as the revenue of the country nosedived. Typically, whenever global oil price declines, Nigeria's oil revenue declines, and so does the country's expenditure.

The rentier thesis posits further that because resource revenues are sufficient to keep the rentier government functioning, the government becomes reluctant to tax its citizens. As argued by Mahdavy (1970, p. 432), oil rent 'enables the governments of the oil producing countries to embark on large public expenditure programmes without resorting to taxation'. Beblawi (1987, pp. 53–54) lends credence to this assertion, remarking that the oil-rentier government's budget 'remains a one-sided document, an expenditure programme, a promise to spend money and distribute benefits to the population with virtually no levy on them in terms of taxes or similar impositions'. These are true descriptions of the oil-rich Arab countries. However, unlike these countries, the Nigerian state extracts taxes from its citizens but proceeds from these sources constitute a negligible component of national revenue. Since the Nigerian rentier state is less dependent on taxation, it, therefore, follows that oil rents reduce the economic significance of the Nigerian taxpayer.

It has been variously suggested also that the abundance of natural resources is closely linked to political instability, especially in an ethnically divided society like Nigeria (Brass 2008; Collier and Hoeffler 1998; Ross 1999, 2001). The argument here is that sharing of resource spoils has the tendency to cause resentment among certain sections of the country and this may result in conflict or civil war. Some studies, however, have provided a contrary view to the resource-conflict nexus. For example, Smith (2004, p. 232) argued that 'oil wealth is robustly associated with increased regime durability … and with lower likelihoods of civil war and anti-state protest', so instead of oil wealth undermining regime viability, it may actually enhance its durability. Smith's assertion is based on his research of the effects of oil wealth on political stability, which drew on cross-sectional time series data from 107 countries in the developing world between 1960 and 1999. This counter-argument notwithstanding, it is clear that the unhealthy competition for Nigeria's oil wealth has contributed to its political instability.

As we have seen in Nigeria, unequal distribution of resources can cause conflict when left-out groups choose violence in an attempt to force redistribution. In her study of Nigeria's coup d'états, Turner (1978) links the polity's instability to the distribution of oil resources. Turner developed a model called a 'commercial triangle' to argue that the competition for oil-generated revenue was at the root of some coup d'états in Nigeria. Present in this triangle is the businessman who represents the multinational corporation; the local middleman from the national private sector; and the state official who assists the foreign businessman in gaining access to the local market (pp. 167–172). Turner used the 1975 coup that ousted General Gowon from office as an empirical justification for her theoretical construct, contending that Gowon's regime was overthrown because the monopolisation of oil policy by state officials did not go down well with those left out of decision making. Although leaders of the coup claimed that they toppled the regime in order to save the country's collapsing economy, analysts argue that intra-military problems were the reason for the coup, thereby vindicating Turner's claim (Collin et al. 1976, p. 185; Osaghae 1998, p. 80). General Murtala Mohammed, who replaced Gowon as head of state, was said to allege that the affairs of the state, supposedly a collective responsibility, were characterised by a lack of consultation, and neglect (quoted in Collin et al. 1976, p. 185). In other words, those outside the triangle felt they were left out and had to remove those within.

Rentier scholars are of the view that natural resource endowments exert a significant influence on the institutions of the state. The argument here is that if the right institutions are put in place, resources can bring about economic growth and a stable polity, and overall, be a blessing. Karl (1997), for example, contends that resource abundance has the tendency to weaken state institutions. Specifically, Karl argues that oil windfalls cause petro-states to suffer from short-sightedness, as 'rational oligopoly and sterilisation rapidly lose out to "petromania"' (pp. 66–67). This short-sightedness makes the states try to do too much too soon, thereby giving rise to the state becoming overextended (Karl 1997, pp. 66–67; Auty and Gelb 2001, p. 132). This is the case with the Nigerian state which has become so overextended that it finds it increasingly difficult to provide public goods for its citizens as well as balance its budgets.

Rentier thesis also holds that the abundance of oil rents enables rentier states to embark on massive public expenditure programmes, especially in the non-tradable sectors such as construction. Of course, one would expect public spending to stimulate economic growth but this has not been the case in Nigeria because expenditure has not been geared towards a productive activity or genuine developmental projects. This reinforces the view that resource-rich countries invest badly, with too many white elephant projects (Collier 2008, p. 44). In Nigeria, oil rents are spent on unviable projects as well as on patronage. Although it may be argued that not all public expenditure in Nigeria is unviable, it is still easy to contend that most public projects are only embarked upon in an attempt to attract or reward political loyalty.

Evidence also suggests that resource abundance has the tendency to result in excessive centralisation, in which the state plays a central role in distributing its resource-generated wealth. In Nigeria, as oil rents flow into the national coffers, the federal government becomes increasingly centralised, and the constituent units correspondingly become financially dependent on the federal government. Sometimes, power, in a rentier state tends to be centralised around a clique or around the office and the person of the president, like in Djibouti where the president unilaterally makes laws and policies (Brass 2008, p. 529). This political control extends to the economy, in which the president is said to be an active participant in virtually all rent-earning activities in the country.

Corruption as an Aspect of the Political Economy

One significant aspect of Nigeria's political economy is corruption. The availability of oil rents seems to make corruption inevitable. Corruption is not limited to any particular society, but it is widespread in Nigeria and has almost become a subculture. The table shows Nigeria's position on the Transparency International's (TI) Corruption Perceptions Index in the Fourth Republic (Table 3.2).

Table 3.2 Nigeria's Corruption Perceptions Index (CPI), 1998–2017

Year	*Number of countries surveyed*	*Country rank*	*CPI score (%)*
1998	85	81	19
1999	99	98	16
2000	90	90	12
2001	91	90	10
2002	102	101	16
2003	133	132	14
2004	145	144	16
2005	158	152	19
2006	163	142	22
2007	179	147	22
2008	180	121	27
2009	180	130	25
2010	178	134	24
2011	183	143	24
2012	176	139	27
2013	177	144	25
2014	175	136	27
2015	168	136	26
2016	176	136	28
2017	180	148	27

Source Adapted from the Transparency International's Corruption Perceptions Index

Typically, the rentier state is a locus of pervasive corruption by the political elites and other rent seekers. With the transformation of the Nigerian state into a distributive state, oil wealth distribution becomes central to politics. One feature of a rentier state is that resource wealth tends to be concentrated in the hands of the few who then constitute themselves into a rentier class. In Nigeria, the rentier class are those state officials who are in control of oil resources. It needs to be reiterated here that the rentier class does not engage in the production of wealth; it only involves itself in the distribution of wealth. As a social group, rentiers are unproductive, sharing in the produce. (Beblawi 1987, p. 50). Rather than engaging in the actual production of wealth, the business elite in Nigeria prefer to serve as junior partners to the multinational companies. These business/political elites finance party activities and in turn reap the reward in the form of contract award.

As Karl (1997, p. 57) pointed out, oil wealth tends to produce a 'rentier psychology', a situation that 'rewards those who can "milk the cow" without effort rather than those engaged in less remunerative but more productive activities'. Karl argues further that booms exacerbate existing rent-seeking behaviour as well as create such behaviour where it did not already exist. It is difficult not to agree that oil wealth has made patronage and rent-seeking more widespread in Nigeria, with officeholders believing they are in office to satisfy themselves and their clients. Of course, patronage politics had been a feature of Nigerian politics even before the introduction of oil into the country's economy, only that massive inflow of oil rents, especially since the oil boom period significantly deepened the level. As mentioned earlier, before oil, the regional marketing boards were the main avenues through which state officeholders enriched themselves. According to Welch (1995, p. 636), 'Nigeria has received billions of dollars from oil – most of which seems to have disappeared into private hands without perceptible benefit to most Nigerians'. This explains why politics in Nigeria is warfare; a matter of life and death.

Another feature of a rentier state is a lack of accountability in government. Beblawi and Luciani (1987, p. 7) note that oil revenues enable the state to 'buy off political consensus', or in the case of Nigeria, to 'settle the opposition'. During boom periods, rentier governments tend to placate important or vocal social groups with oil revenues. In 1975, in an attempt to curry public support for the then military regime, the government increased wages by about 100% and also gave workers generous benefits. The move led to inflation. Similarly, the use of oil revenue to 'settle' members of the society during the Babangida and Abacha military era was second to none.

Since the rentier state is the 'distributor of favours and benefits', officeholders find it convenient to award contracts as an expression of gratitude rather than as a reflection of economic rationale (Beblawi 1987, p. 55). In Nigeria, the most common avenue for corruption can be found in procurement contracts. Usually, contractors collude with state officials to inflate contracts and the officials take the extra profit. Sometimes, office holders deliberately propose unviable projects so that they can make fortunes for themselves.

Another avenue through which corrupt practices take place is the siphoning of public funds meant for constituency projects. With the re-establishment of democratic rule in 1999, there arose the need for legislators both at the federal and state levels to provide some 'dividends of democracy' to their constituents. Nigeria consists of 360 federal constituencies, and every constituency is expected to enjoy some measure of government presence by having some projects sited in each. The idea of a constituency project came about as a result of the need to ensure a fair distribution of infrastructure in all parts of the country. However, there are blatant deviations from the main objective of the scheme as legislators use a substantial part of the funds meant for projects for their personal enrichment. More often than not, projects are either not executed or executed halfway, and where they were executed, they were poorly done. Clearly, the constituency project initiative is a laudable one; however, it is based on a wrong premise in the sense that a lawmaker should have no business with project execution. This is the function of the executive arm of government. A large number of the identified projects under the scheme are those that should be executed by the state and local governments. Another shortcoming of the scheme is that the identification of projects, the award of contracts, the supervision and payments for such contracts are left completely in the hands of the legislators, all of which combine to encourage corruption. The citizens for whom the projects are meant for are rarely carried along in the identification of projects, as the legislators act unilaterally to determine the needs of the people.

Corruption, no doubt has a negative impact on the management of public resources. Funds that could have been used to provide public goods are used by state officeholders to cater for themselves and their cronies. Therefore, corruption constitutes a 'leakage' from the economy and distorts economic growth. This has been the case in Nigeria where members of the political elites devote their energy to the pursuit of their narrow interests while the economy is allowed to suffer. Moreover, corruption increases the cost of administration, thereby making governance unnecessarily expensive.

Conclusion

Having examined the political economy of Nigeria within our chosen theoretical standpoint, that is, the rentier thesis, it is convenient to argue that the fundamental character of the contemporary Nigerian political economy is the exploitation and marketing of oil. The chapter has depicted a picture of a political economy suffering from poor economic linkage between resource and non-resource sectors. Rather than utilise the resources generated from oil to initiate the process of economic growth, Nigeria is content with its status as a rentier state. Nigeria's undoing, particularly, since the oil boom era has been its heavy reliance upon oil, and consequent failure to diversify. Despite the enormous inflow of oil rents into the Nigerian economy, the country continues to display poor economic performance.

Earnings from oil, especially in the 1970s provided the federal centre with the financial resources to embark upon some developmental projects, but this also paved the way for the rent-seeking elements of the state to amass wealth for themselves. Rents accrued to Nigeria make offices of the state attractive to elites who constitute themselves into a rentier class, wherein members compete among themselves for control of the state. Using oil wealth to initiate any form of genuine development would be inimical to the interests of this unproductive class. We have also demonstrated that the instability of the international oil market does have negative impacts on Nigeria's domestic economy. Furthermore, it has been demonstrated that Nigeria's political instability is rooted in its over-dependence on oil. The ruthless struggle for state patronage culminated in the collapse of the country's first attempt at a federal system, which saw the emergence of the military on the political stage and also the collapse of the Second Republic (1979–1983).

In the next chapter, we examine the intrinsic relationship between Nigeria's political economy and the practice of federalism.

References

Aboyade, O. (1966). *Foundations of an African Economy: A Study of Investment and Growth in Nigeria.* New York, Washington, and London: Praeger.

Ake, C. (1981). *A Political Economy of Africa.* Harlow: Longman.

Amin, S. (1981). Underdevelopment and Dependence in Black Africa: Origins and Contemporary Forms. In D. Cohen & J. Daniel (Eds.), *Political Economy of Africa: Selected Readings.* Harlow and Essex: Longman Group Limited.

Auty, R. M., & Gelb, A. (2001). Political Economy of Resource-Abundant States. In R. M. Auty (Ed.), *Resource Abundance and Economic Development.* Oxford: Oxford University Press.

Bangura, Y., Mustapha, A. R., & Adamu, S. (1986). The Deepening Economic Crisis and Its Political Implications. In S. Mohammed & T. Edoh (Eds.), *Nigeria: A Republic in Ruins.* Zaria: Gaskiya Corporation.

Beblawi, H. (1987). The Rentier State in the Arab World. In H. Beblawi & G. Luciani (Eds.), *The Rentier State.* London: Croom Helm.

Beblawi, H., & Luciani, G. (1987). Introduction. In H. Beblawi & G. Luciani (Eds.), *The Rentier State.* London: Croom Helm.

Brass, J. N. (2008). Djibouti's Unusual Resource Curse. *Journal of Modern African Studies, 46*(4), 523–545.

Coleman, J. (1958). *Nigeria: Background to Nationalism*. Los Angeles: University of California Press.

Collier, P. (2008). *The Bottom Billion: Why the Poorest Countries Are Failing and What Can Be Done About It*. Oxford: Oxford University Press.

Collier, P., & Hoeffler, A. (1998). On Economic Causes of Civil War. *Oxford Economic Articles, 50*(4), 563–573.

Collin, P., Turner, T., & Williams, G. (1976). Capitalism and the Coup. In G. Williams (Ed.), *Nigeria: Economy and Society*. London: Rex Collings.

Ejobowah, J. (2010). Territorial Pluralism: Assessing the Ethnofederal Variant in Nigeria. *Regional and Federal Studies, 20*(2), 251–274.

First, F. (1980). Libya: Class and State in an Oil Economy. In P. Nore & T. Turner (Eds.), *Oil and Class Struggle*. London: Zed Press.

Graf, W. (1988). *The Nigerian State: Political Economy, State, Class and Political System in the Post-colonial Era*. London: Currey.

International Crisis Group (ICG). (2006, July 19). *Nigeria: Want in the Midst of Plenty* (Crisis Group Africa Report, No. 113).

Karl, T. (1997). *The Paradox of Plenty: Oil Booms and Petro-States*. Berkeley: University of California Press.

Khan, S. (1994). *Nigeria: The Political Economy of Oil*. Oxford: Oxford University Press.

Kirk-Greene, A. H. M., & Rimmer, D. (1981). *Nigeria Since 1970: A Political and Economic Outline*. London: Hodder & Stoughton.

Luciani, G. (1987). Allocation vs. Production States. In H. Beblawi & G. Luciani (Eds.), *The Rentier State*. London: Croom Helm.

Luciani, G. (Ed.). (1990). *The Arab State*. Berkeley and Los Angeles: University of California Press.

Mahdavy, H. (1970). The Patterns and Problems of Economic Development in Rentier States: The Case of Iran. In M. A. Cook (Ed.), *Studies in The Economic History of The Middle East*. London: Oxford University Press.

Osaghae, E. (1998). *The Crippled Giant: Nigeria Since Independence*. London: Hurst Company.

Rodney, W. (1972). *How Europe Underdeveloped Africa*. London: Bogle-L'Ouverture Publications.

Ross, M. (1999, January). The Political Economy of the Resource Curse. *World Politics, 51*, 279–322, 305–306.

Ross, M. (2001, April). Does Oil Hinder Democracy? *World Politics, 53*, 325–361.

Smith, B. (2004, April). Oil Wealth and Regime Survival in the Developing World, 1960–1999. *American Journal of Political Science, 48*(2), 232–246.

Turner, T. (1978). Commercial Capitalism and the 1975 Coup. In S. K. Panter-Brick (Ed.), *Soldiers and Oil: The Political Transformation of Nigeria*. London: Frank Cass.

Welch, C. (1995). The Ogoni and Self-Determination: Increasing Violence in Nigeria. *Journal of Modern African Studies, 33*(4), 635–649.

White, G., & Taylor, S. (2001). Well-Oiled Regimes: Oil & Uncertain Transitions in Algeria & Nigeria. *Review of African Political Economy, 28*(89), 323–344.

Williams, G. (1976). Nigeria: A Political Economy. In G. Williams (Ed.), *Nigeria: Economy and Society*. London: Rex Collings.

Yates, D. (1996). *The Rentier State in Africa: Oil Rent Dependency and Neocolonialism in the Republic of Gabon*. Trenton: Africa World Press.

CHAPTER 4

Revenue Allocation in Nigeria

Introduction

Typically, revenue sharing in a federal state is a complex task because both the federal and constituent governments are in competition for the federation's limited resources. In Nigeria, the practice of sharing nationally-generated revenue predates the formation of the federation in 1954. The practice began under the unitary Richards Constitution of 1946, which regionalised the country into three 'compartments'. Since then, the revenue allocation system has been characterised by some continuity and change. There was a semblance of continuity in the system between 1946 until 1966 when the military stormed the political stage. That phase in the political history of the country was largely characterised by a strong periphery and a weak federal centre. This, however, changed during the military era which coincided with the oil boom era. Military rule facilitated the transformation of the previously peripheralised federation into a highly centralised one. As presently constituted, Nigeria operates a top-down federal system in which the federal government determines which tier of government gets what share of the national revenue.

The practice of what has been referred to as 'federal finance' in classical federal studies or 'fiscal federalism' in contemporary federal studies varies from federation to federation. However, the common feature is that it delineates the sharing of a federation's national wealth. Fiscal federalism broadly addresses two fundamental questions: One, what tax should be collected by which tier of government? Two, how should the

D. Babalola, *The Political Economy of Federalism in Nigeria*, Federalism and Internal Conflicts,
https://doi.org/10.1007/978-3-030-05493-9_4

nationally-collected taxes be shared among the different tiers of government? Nigeria's fiscal federalism, just like those of other federations, is also characterised by revenue sharing amongst the three tiers of government—federal, state and local governments. In the same way, the revenue allocation system revolves around three main problems: the problem of allocation of revenue to the different tiers in relation to their constitutionally assigned functions (vertical revenue sharing); the problem of sharing of revenue among the states and local governments (horizontal revenue sharing); and the problem of allocation of the oil-generated revenue between the oil-producing states and the non oil-producing ones. These issues have dominated the country's fiscal system, and by extension, the practice of federalism. In spite of the fact that the assignment of responsibilities and sharing of the centrally-generated revenues are entrenched in the constitution, revenue allocation has not ceased to be a contentious issue. The vertical revenue sharing attracts less acrimony, perhaps because it has been accepted by all parties in the sharing arrangement that the central government is entitled to the most lucrative sources of revenue. The horizontal sharing, however, has been more problematic partly because of the economic disparity characterising the states but mainly because of the excessive concentration of resources at the centre.

This chapter provides an understanding of fiscal federalism (revenue allocation system) from theoretical standpoints with a view to understanding the character of Nigeria's fiscal federalism. The aim is to establish the extent to which Nigeria's revenue allocation system can be said to conform with or deviate from existing theories and practices. In order to achieve this aim, the chapter also addresses the theoretical issues of tax and expenditure assignments within federations, as well as the rationale for intergovernmental transfers. Moreover, the chapter also examines the underlying principles and their application in revenue sharing in Nigeria. In doing so, it focuses on the politics, as well as the economics around revenue sharing. The key argument in this chapter is that the federal government's pre-eminent role in the distribution of the country's resources, particularly the oil-generated revenue, contributes to the acrimonious inter-governmental relations that have become a feature of the system. In Nigeria, federal-state relations have been more of antagonism than cooperation. Since the country's return to civilian rule in 1999, there have been several conflicts involving either the federal government and the states or the states and the local governments. Over-centralisation of the system, which has resulted from over-dependence on oil, is the major source of the problem bedevilling Nigeria. The chapter, therefore, starts with the meaning of fiscal federalism.

Fiscal Federalism: Towards an Understanding

Fiscal federalism is concerned with the sharing of fiscal resources in a federation. It is basically about revenue allocation in a federal system of government. According to Oates (1999, p. 1120), fiscal federalism addresses the vertical structure of the public sector, as well as explores the roles of the different levels of government including the ways of their relationship through such instruments as inter-government grants. Likewise, for Freinkman (2008, p. 153), fiscal federalism 'defines the core rules for resource allocation, distribution of responsibilities for service delivery, and mechanisms for interaction between different tiers of government'. What we find easy to deduce from the above definitions is that fiscal federalism is simply about resource distribution in a federation and is vital to the practice of federalism.

An essential aspect of fiscal federalism is how to ensure that the sharing of revenue between federal and state governments corresponds with the distribution of constitutional functions. Some federations establish an independent body or commission to operate their fiscal system. In Nigeria, an independent fiscal body, the National Revenue Mobilisation, Allocation and Fiscal Commission (NRMAFC), established in 1989, reviews the revenue-sharing formula and also advises the presidency on the sharing of national revenues. Section 162(2) of the 1999 Constitution also empowers the President of Nigeria to table a revenue formula before the National Assembly regularly upon receipt of advice from the NRMAFC. Unlike the previous fiscal commissions, the NRMAFC is a permanent body. It is also independent, at least in theory.

If we accept that fiscal federalism is about intergovernmental fiscal relations in a federation, then it should not be difficult to accept that fiscal federalism is an offshoot of federalism, which is itself a sub-field of political science. For some economists, however, fiscal federalism is within the arena of economics as it is concerned with public finance. The question, therefore, is, is fiscal federalism a political or an economic matter? Some scholars, mostly economists, emphasise economic objectives as the only factors underpinning intergovernmental fiscal relations in federal countries, whilst underplaying the politics involved in such relations.[1] For these scholars, the allocations of taxing powers and expenditures, and the use of intergovernmental transfers to achieve the objectives of economic efficiency and equity are the crux of fiscal federalism. According to Phillips (1971), constitution-makers should be saddled with the responsibility of rationally allocating functions while fiscal experts concentrate on how to allocate taxing powers and how to share revenue between governments in the federation.[2] Of course, there is no denying that the primary motivation behind the formation of many federations is economic but it should not be forgotten that a federation is a political creation. Thus, studying a federation's fiscal system without due cognisance to its politics may be misleading.

To some political scientists, fiscal federalism is fundamentally a political matter. Watts (2003), for example, argued that intergovernmental fiscal arrangements are not mere technical adjustments but 'inevitably the result of *political compromises*', and constitute a vital aspect of a federation's *political* operation (p. 2). In the same fashion, Aiyede (2009, p. 252) argued that fiscal federalism is a political matter that is central to the success or failure of the federal project as it involves a constant struggle between the central and the constituent unit actors for the distribution of authority. Another set of political scientists is of the view that the issue of revenue allocation is both economic and political in nature. For instance, Oyediran and Olagunju (1979, p. 211) argued that revenue allocation is 'strictly an economic issue' but with 'a high political content', so ignoring the politics of revenue allocation is misleading.[3]

Clearly, the foregoing debate shows that economic objectives cannot be divorced from political objectives in any federal fiscal relation. The economic and political variables within a federation must not be ignored if one is to fully understand the character of the federation's fiscal system.

[1] Scholars such as Richard Musgrave, Wallace Oates, Richard Bird, Anwar Shah and Robin Boadway are in this category.

[2] Adedotun Phillips was a professor of economics and has written extensively on the Revenue allocation system in Nigeria. He was also a member of the Revenue Allocation Commission established in 1979.

[3] Oyeleye Oyediran and Olatunji Olagunju are eminent professors of political science in Nigeria.

The dynamic interrelationship between these variables is crucial to the successful operation of the federal system. Understanding a federation's fiscal system requires an understanding of the political context within which the fiscal system operates. Fiscal matters, especially in a multi-ethnic federation such as Nigeria, go beyond the purview of economics as they have also assumed political dimension. Generally, as Burgess (2006, p. 148) argued, fiscal federalism is a function of the national political economy, highlighting the fundamental aspects of a federation. Likewise, a former chair of NRMAFC, retired army General T. Y. Danjuma, once remarked that the issue of revenue allocation falls squarely within the area of political economy as it is 'partly economic, but largely a matter of political compromise' (Danjuma 1996, p. 89). In other words, fiscal federalism should be treated as a political economy matter.

Arguments for Intergovernmental Transfers

This section addresses the arguments for intergovernmental transfers but it is imperative to discuss the general nature of intergovernmental grants before discussing the rationales behind them. Federations such as Austria, Germany, and Nigeria, heavily favour revenue sharing, whereas, the federations of Australia, Belgium, and Spain, for example, adopt the use of revenue sharing and fiscal transfers. In Canada, Switzerland, and the United States, where the constituent units have significant own-source revenues, transfers from the federal centre constitute the main form of fiscal support to the constituent units (Anderson 2010; Awa 1976; Oates 1999).

Intergovernmental grants can be classified into two main categories: general-purpose or unconditional; and specific-purpose or conditional grants. An unconditional grant is usually a lump-sum transfer that does not have any spending strings attached and may be used as desired by the recipient government, usually the constituent government (Ashwe 1986, p. 4; Boadway and Shah 2009, p. 307; Iyoha 2008, p. 197). These transfers are typically mandated by law and are meant to augment the recipient's own resources. Unconditional transfer fulfils two related objectives: one, to close the fiscal gap in federating units with low revenue-raising capacity; and two, to bring about some form of equalisation among the federating units. In ideal federal financial setups, the use of unconditional grants enables the transfer of funds from wealthy constituent units to the less wealthy ones, thereby bringing about a sense of equality among the constituent units. In Australia and Canada, for example, the central governments make unconditional grants available to the constituent units for equalisation purposes as poorer jurisdictions get more funds per capita (Oates 1972, p. 78). Similarly, in India, the main financial support for the states from the federal government comes through unconditional shares of federal taxes (Anderson 2010, p. 60). Unconditional grants are usually based upon the fiscal characteristics of the recipient government, such as fiscal capacity or revenue-raising capacity, fiscal need or fiscal effort.

Conditional grants are supplementary transfers to constituent units, and they are meant for specific purposes. In other words, they must be spent as directed by the granting government, usually the federal government. This form of transfer typically specifies the type of expenditure that can be financed with the grant. In some cases, the receiving constituent unit may be required to match federal financial support with a specified percentage of expenditures using their own resources. This is called matching requirement, and the grant provided is called cost-shared grant. This requirement encourages the scrutiny, as well as local ownership of grant-financed projects (Boadway and Shah 2009, p. 309). Another form of conditional grant is the contributory grant, which usually covers all of the costs of a constituent unit's programme that the federal government wishes to see implemented (Anderson 2010, p. 60). The conditions attached notwithstanding, conditional grants provide the needed financial support for constituent units enabling them to undertake specific programmes that have high priority in the overall economy of the federation. Another advantage of conditional grants is that they may be used to bring about desirable minimum standards for certain services such as education and health (Awa 1976, p. 73). Also, as mentioned earlier, since they aim at particular objectives, it is relatively easy to check the expenditure performance of any recipient government.

One major argument against conditional grants is that the recipient's independence becomes limited upon receiving these grants. Another argument is that since the recipient is restricted in the use of the grant, it may end up focusing excessively on the agreed project at the expense of other equally important projects. Key to these arguments is that these limitations amount to encroachment in the affairs of the recipient government, and may lead to a situation where the recipient becomes subordinated to the federal government. These arguments have no basis, especially where co-operative federalism, that is, a genuine partnership between the federal and state governments exists. Inter-dependence in every sphere of a federal system is crucial to the successful operation of the system. According to Vile (1961, p. 176), the American federal system gives room for this type of cooperative project without the states becoming subordinate to the central government. Moreover, the system allows rich constituent governments who want to avoid the danger of subordination to reject federal grants if they wish.

Grants, be they conditional or unconditional, play vital roles in the fiscal operations of federal states. They have the capacity to enable or constrain governments in the exercise of their constitutionally assigned responsibilities (Watts 1999, p. 43). Federations use both forms of grant depending on the objectives and priorities of the national government. The use of conditional grants has been favoured in Austria, Germany, and the United States because the emphasis in these countries is on fiscal responsibility at the constituent unit level. Nigeria's federal system emphasises the maximisation of state, thereby making the use of unconditional grants a norm. In Nigeria, the central government is required by law to make regular grants available to the state governments. Specifically, the states receive two kinds of allocation—statutory and non-statutory. With regards to the statutory allocation, Section 162(3) of the Nigerian Constitution of 1999 requires the federal government to make unconditional grants available to the states on an annual basis to enable them to discharge their constitutional responsibilities. Non-statutory grants are usually given to a state facing an emergency situation such as natural disaster, terrorist acts, conflicts and similar problems. Grants constitute a primary source of revenue for state governments in Nigeria, whereas, they are supposed to supplement states' internally generated revenue.

Let us turn our attention to the arguments for intergovernmental transfers. A federation must possess the capacity to operate itself. What this means is that both the general and constituent governments must possess sufficient economic resources to finance their respective activities. Each must be self-financing to ensure also some measure of fiscal autonomy. Wheare (1963, p. 93), for example, argued that if the federal principle is to operate in law and in practice, both the general and regional governments must possess adequate financial resources to enable them perform their individual functions (see also, Maddox 1941; Watts 1966). It is, however, common, especially in developing federations, for some constituent units to experience fiscal gap whereby their spending responsibilities exceed their ability to raise revenue.

Irrespective of how it happens, a vertical fiscal gap has to be filled by either conditional or unconditional grants, or both. Otherwise, the state may experience fiscal imbalance. Coming to the aid of a distressed state is a standard practice in federal countries. If the national economy is to operate at its optimum level, and if the federation is to avoid instability, the central government must deal with the fiscal imbalance in any region. Fiscal imbalance in one region may have a contagious effect on other regions. However, it is difficult to measure the degree of fiscal gap, especially in a developing federation such as Nigeria, because it has become the norm for every state to experience a fiscal gap in its budget. In an ideal federation, the most realistic yardstick for measuring the size of fiscal gap would be 'fiscal capacity', 'need', and 'effort' (Ashwe 1986; Watts 2003). Fiscal capacity or revenue raising capacity refers to the ability of a government to raise revenues based on its potential revenue sources in order to finance public services. Constituent units with relatively rich resources generally have greater fiscal capacities. Grants based on the relative fiscal capacity of recipient governments are referred to as revenue-equalisation grants (Ashwe 1986, p. 4). Fiscal need refers to any special circumstances which may require higher per capita expenditures in one jurisdiction relative to another. For example, a constituent unit with a high proportion of school-age children in its population will incur higher per capita educational expenditures than one with a lower proportion. Grants meant to equalise the fiscal need of recipient governments are referred to as 'expenditure-equalisation transfers' (Ashwe 1986, p. 5). Fiscal effort refers to the extent to which the government is able to exploit its potential tax bases.

There seems to be a consensus on the view that inter-governmental grants are instruments of fiscal adjustment and that they are meant to achieve certain political and economic objectives. According to Adedeji (1969, p. 220), fiscal adjustment in a federation is usually necessitated by four main factors: the problem of resolving the imbalance of resources and needs between the federal and regional governments; the problem of harmonising income with needs in the different regions; the need to ensure that 'economic equilibrium' is achieved for the federation as a whole; and the need to 'level up' so that the poorer regions are raised and the level of services provided in the different regions is equalised. Similarly, Oates (1999, p. 1126) argued that as a policy instrument in fiscal federalism, inter-governmental grants can serve a number of functions, including: the internalisation of spill-over benefit to other jurisdictions; fiscal equalisation across jurisdictions; and an improved overall tax system. These views are corroborated by Watts (2003, p. 1) who noted that the problem of distribution of resources in a federation revolves around such issues as: the correction of vertical financial imbalances between expenditure responsibilities and financial resources; pressures for equalisation to correct horizontal imbalances; the need for coordination of taxing powers; the need for regular adjustment of financial arrangements; and the relation of all of these to the political setting, institutions and processes of the country concerned.

Inter-governmental grants are usually designed to achieve the objective of fiscal equity or equality among the states of a federation. Fiscal equity here refers to equality in the fiscal capacity of the units that constitute the federation. In fiscal federalism, two notions of equity are usually identified: vertical equity and horizontal equity. The former deals with the problem of fiscal treatment of the unequal, that is, how to ensure a progressive income tax; while horizontal equity is concerned with the treatment of equals, which emphasises that persons in like circumstances in two parts of the country ought to be treated the same by their respective public sectors (Ashwe 1986, p. 8). The problem, however, is how to define equity or equality among politically similar units of a given federation. This problem is partly at the heart of revenue sharing in Nigeria. Lack of definition notwithstanding, horizontal equity is unattainable in a developing federation like Nigeria because of the degree of economic disparity. Thus, the case for the use of unconditional grants aimed at equalising the ability of all sub-national units in the federation to provide the required public services for their citizens becomes tenable. Grants of this kind are usually referred to as 'equalisation' grants because their primary function is to correct a sub-national government's fiscal deficiency (Olaloku 1979, p. 110). It is important to note that, although richer component units have contributed more into the national coffer they still receive the same per-capita grant as the poorer constituent, and in spite of this, equalisation has taken place.

A further argument for inter-governmental grants revolves around what is referred to in the literature as 'inter-jurisdictional spill-over'. It is usually the practice in federations for every constituent government to provide mainly for the citizens within its jurisdiction, but it is possible for the services provided to benefit the citizens of neighbouring constituent units. According to Ashwe (1986, p. 6), an inter-jurisdictional spill-over exists when 'public sector activity in one jurisdiction provides benefits to or imposes costs on the residents of other jurisdictions'. For example, expenditure for public services such as hospitals, highways, and educational institutions may generate spill-over effects. In an attempt to satisfy their citizens, sub-national governments do ignore the costs of spill-over while providing certain services. Conditional grants are therefore required to take care of the spill-over costs. Grants of this nature can be considered as subsidies meant to encourage particular sub-national governments in their development efforts. By implication, therefore, these grants can only be spent on public activities that result in incurring some spill-over costs at the constituent level.

Tax Assignment in Nigeria

It is important to start this section with a discussion of how fiscal transfers are designed before discussing the assignment of taxes. In designing fiscal transfers, certain factors must be given consideration. The first factor is that of 'administrative efficiency'. This implies that taxing powers should be assigned to the tier of government most likely to administer them efficiently, that is, with minimum tax efforts or costs. Usually, the federal government is considered more efficient in collecting certain taxes. Likewise, because the federating units are closer to the people, taxes with local impact (tax sources that would allow them to provide for the citizens within their jurisdictions) are assignable to them. State governments are usually assigned tax sources that do not endanger national macroeconomic policy; taxes that are relatively inexpensive to administer; and have relatively stable yields (Suberu 2001, p. 47).

Another factor worth considering is that of 'fiscal independence'. This criterion stipulates that each tier of government should raise revenues in a manner that preserves their autonomy (Ekpo 2006, p. 214; Galadima 2008, p. 62). A federal fiscal system must also take cognisance of the 'adequacy and stability' of the resources available to all the governments in the federation. This principle implies that the revenue sharing practice must ensure that 'available resources are elastic enough to meet the expanding needs of the governments', and their sources must also be stable, particularly for the sub-national governments (Phillips 1971, p. 389). The sub-national governments should have adequate revenues that would enable them to discharge their constitutional responsibilities. The issue of 'equity' or fairness is also important to a grant design. As suggested by Boadway and Shah (2009, p. 352), allocated funds should vary directly with fiscal need factors and inversely with the tax capacity of each jurisdiction. 'Predictability' is another factor that should not be ignored in designing fiscal transfers. Sub-national governments should be able to predict expected income from the federal transfer. This allows them to plan against expected revenue and also devise a coping mechanism when there is a shortfall. Moreover, the design of fiscal transfer should have some element of 'responsiveness and flexibility'. Fiscal systems must be able to respond to 'unforeseen changes in the fiscal situation of the recipients' (Boadway and Shah 2009, p. 352). The system must be flexible enough to allow sub-national governments to adjust to any shortfall in the revenue base of the central government.

It is important to point out that these factors are in conflict with each other. For instance, the principle of fiscal efficiency allows the central government to dominate major taxes, such as import and export taxes, making fiscal independence almost impossible. Unfortunately, in Nigeria, the efficiency criterion has always been favoured. A major argument in favour of the federal government collecting most revenue is that the federal government is bigger in size and more efficient in collecting major taxes. Nigeria has consistently assigned the most lucrative sources of revenue to the federal government, while the less important ones go to the state governments. The underlying assumption that underpins this financial arrangement is that the functions assigned to the central government require more funds than those assigned to the states. This is an erroneous assumption, especially where such subjects as health care and education assigned to state governments also require a lot of funding. Also, the principle of 'adequacy and stability' allows the federal government to raise more revenue than the sub-national governments, consequently leading to federal supremacy in fiscal matters.

How are expenditure responsibilities assigned in a typical federation? States, be they federal or unitary, perform three main functions—allocation, distribution, and stabilisation. It is common to discuss the assignment of responsibilities in a federal system within the context of these functions. A significant feature of a federal system is the constitutional assignment of responsibilities between the tiers of government within the federation. The allocation function refers to the provision of public goods for the benefit of all citizens in the country. The fiscal federalism literature provides that public goods and services should be provided by local governments when their benefits accrue to a local population and by central government when the benefits accrue to the country as a whole. As suggested by Oates (1972, p. 54), sub-national governments should provide goods and services whose consumption is limited to their geographical areas of competence in the interest of efficiency and welfare maximisation. The distribution function of a state refers to those activities undertaken by a government to bring about equality in income and wealth, and most scholars of fiscal federalism are in consensus that this function is better performed by the central government (Oates 1999, p. 1121). The stabilisation function requires the use of fiscal instruments such as money supply, and balance of payments to achieve the macroeconomic objectives of economic growth and ultimately a stable economy for the country as a whole. According to Oates (1999, p. 1121), the classical theory of fiscal federalism contends that the central government should have the basic responsibility for the macroeconomic stabilisation function and for income redistribution. Like the distribution function, the central government is the only tier that can be entrusted with the stabilisation function. While the central government performs the distribution and stabilisation functions, the allocation function should be jointly performed by both the central and sub-national governments.

As noted above, two factors usually influence the distribution of responsibilities among the different tiers of government: the benefits from collective action; and economies of scale (Anderson 2010, pp. 9–18; Awa 1976, p. 62; Ekpo 2006, p. 210; Galadima 2008, pp. 57–58). Thus, the federal government should be assigned those functions that benefit the whole national population, and those of local nature should be assigned to state and local governments. By implication, therefore, the federal government should provide such goods and services as policing and defence, because these benefits every citizen in the country. Moreover, functions that can be more efficiently performed by the federal government should be placed in the exclusive list, and those whose benefits are more local should be in the concurrent list.

In Nigeria, matters of foreign affairs and national defence are exclusively the responsibilities of the federal government. These functions benefit the entire country, and in addition, they can be more efficiently performed by the federal government. Besides, they require enormous funding. Defence, for example, is linked closely to the country's security, and such an important item should not be left in the hands of a constituent government. The state governments have responsibility for education, health, provision of public utilities and such other items that benefit citizens in their jurisdictions.

How are the taxes assigned in Nigeria? In most federations, the federal government is typically in control of the lucrative tax jurisdictions leaving the states with the less lucrative ones. In Mexico, Nigeria, and Russia, for example, federal revenues are around 90% of the total; between 70 and 85% in Australia and Belgium; 60–65% in Austria and Germany; and about 55% in the United States (Anderson 2010, p. 21). Given the enormity of the functions of the federal government, it is rational for that government to be assigned a greater proportion of national revenues. However, sub-national governments should have an independent revenue base to enable them to raise the needed resources to discharge their governmental responsibilities. Having an independent revenue base tends to translate into fiscal autonomy.

In Nigeria, the federal government collects import and export duties, corporation tax, value-added tax (VAT), excise duties, mining rents and royalties, petroleum profit tax, and personal income tax from the armed forces, police and residents of the Federal Capital Territory (FCT). Proceeds from these taxes are shared with the states. In most federations, the federal government plays an important role in the collection of corporation taxes. Canada and the United States, for example, do permit the two tiers of government access to corporation taxes, whereas, in Nigeria, this is exclusive to the federal government. The reason for the centrality of the federal governments in the issue of corporation tax, according to Anderson (2010, p. 35), is that 'the administrative complexity of dealing with corporations that operate in many parts of the federation further strengthens the case for centralised, or strongly harmonised, design and administration of corporate taxes'. The collection of income taxes differs from federation to federation. For example, the federal government in the United States dominates income taxes, whereas, in Switzerland, these taxes are collected about equally by communes, cantons, and the federal government (Anderson 2010, p. 34). In Nigeria, historically, the federal government is given exclusive jurisdiction over customs and excise. The reasons for this, as Awa (1976, p. 65) argued, are both political and economic, and the argument is worth reproducing in detail:

> From the political point of view it is clear that if the units were allowed to impose and collect the customs and excise duties, they might do so at differential rates and create the impression of having sovereign status vis-a-vis the position of the central government. The union might look more like a

> confederation than a federation. From the economic point of view, there is firstly a desire to ensure a uniform rate of customs and excise duties and a free flow of commodities among the units. There is secondly an attempt to place in the hands of the federal government a reliable source of revenue so that it can, without too much difficulty, meet the demands of preserving the territorial integrity of the federation and the internal constitutional order.

Typically, the central governments in federal countries collect taxes and then distribute the proceeds to constituent governments according to some agreed formula. This is not different in Nigeria where Section 162(1) of the 1999 Constitution provides that the federal government deposits all centrally collected revenues into a general pool, called the Federation Account, to be shared vertically and horizontally. It is important to stress that states and local governments keep their internally generated revenues. In Austria and Germany, fiscal federalism is characterised overwhelmingly by revenue sharing, with constituent units having very limited independent own-source revenue (Anderson 2010, p. 55). Conversely, in Canada, Switzerland and the United States, constituent units control their tax revenues, with negligible or no revenue sharing (but some fiscal transfers), and in Australia, in addition to fiscal transfers, states share all of the federally levied VAT (Anderson 2010, p. 55). In Nigeria, the states' sources of revenue are less lucrative compared with those of the federal government. They are also not adequate to match their constitutional responsibilities. Therefore, the states are left with no option but to depend on the centre in order to bridge their fiscal gap. Local governments generate revenue from liquor sales, birth and death registrations, environmental violations and fines, motor parking dues, and market stalls dues. These sources are many but they are usually inadequate to match local governments' assigned functions, hence their reliance on the federal government. This culture of fiscal dependence on the centre characterises Nigeria's fiscal federalism.

Horizontal Revenue Sharing

Nigeria has adopted a myriad of principles for horizontal sharing of nationally generated revenue. However, the principles of 'derivation', 'need', 'equality', and 'national interest' are applied almost consistently. The principle of derivation, as argued by Boadway and Shah (2009, p. 294), allows transfer of revenue to states where the revenues were raised in the federation. Likewise, for Anderson (2010, p. 54), the principle is about sharing nationally-generated revenue in such a way that revenues raised in a jurisdiction stays there and provide a net benefit for the people of that jurisdiction. In other words, derivation requires the central government to return to the state governments the total, or a proportion, of the taxes that their citizens had paid, or the revenue generated from that state. In Nigeria, the problem of revenue sharing has always revolved around what proportion of the centrally-collected revenue should be returned to the source states. This problem has become a feature of Nigeria's fiscal federalism. As we shall see, the application of this principle has generated the most controversy.

The principle of 'need' is based on the fiscal need of a sub-national government, usually determined by the unit's population. This principle allows for allocation of revenues in relation to the needs of the people in each constituent unit, irrespective of their contribution to total national revenues. The main problem with this principle is how to measure the need of a particular sub-national unit. Using population as an index of need in a multi-ethnic federation such as Nigeria has the tendency to result in abuse of census.

Another principle typically adopted in Nigeria is that of 'equality of states'. This principle is based upon the assumption that all federating units within a federation are equal regardless of population and land mass. So irrespective of their contribution to the national revenue pot, every federating unit is required to be treated equally by receiving equal shares of centrally generated revenues (Elaigwu 2007, p. 206). Adopting this principle has led to clamours by ethno-regional groups for the creation of more states in the country ostensibly because of the expected benefits from the revenue allocation system.

The last is the principle of 'national interest'. This allows for an annual inter-governmental grant to each sub-national unit on a population basis, for specific purposes which must be in the interest of the country as a whole (Awa 1964, p. 197; Elaigwu 2007, p. 206; Olaloku 1979, p. 115). As observed by Elaigwu (2007, p. 207), this principle emphasises the need to raise the living standard of those people in poorer states above the minimum national standard, as fixed by the country's leaders. The principle also emphasises that the federating units should be given adequate resources in order for the entire federation to achieve a balanced development.

Derivation and Revenue Sharing

The derivation principle first crept into Nigeria's fiscal scheme in 1946 when Sir Sydney Phillipson was appointed sole Fiscal Commissioner to determine how revenues should be allocated to the Regional governments. The 1946 Constitution, though, a unitary constitution, sought to give the then three Regions some measure of financial responsibility as each was to have its own budget to take care of the cost of services provided in the region (Adedeji 1969, p. 49). Hence, each Region had to be provided with funds to enable it to discharge its constitutional duties. In order to achieve these objectives, the Phillipson Commission classified revenues into regional (declared) and non-regional revenues (non-declared). Regional revenues were such revenues identifiable within the Region and locally collected by regional authorities and these included direct taxes, licensing fees, mining rents and rents from government properties (Adedeji 1969, pp. 51–52). These revenues constituted what can be referred to as a Region's 'independent revenues'. Non-regional revenues were exclusively the central government's revenues, and these were revenues from export, import, and excise duties.

In addition, the Commission also identified two main principles for distributing non-declared revenues: the principle of derivation; and the principle of even progress. The former was aimed at inculcating a sense of financial responsibility in the Regions in order to enhance their fiscal strength. The principle of even progress was to allow Regions to make up for what they lost under derivation as poor Regions were to receive more than their proportionate share of central revenues. In its recommendation, the Commission arrived at the following allocation formula: Northern Region: 46%; Western Region: 30%; and Eastern Region: 24% (Ashwe 1986, p. 28).

Phillipson's fiscal arrangement became contentious among the Regions. One major criticism against the scheme was that due to lack of reliable statistical data, it was difficult to ascertain what was derived from each Region, especially, with regard to the three major components of non-declared revenues: import and export duties; company tax; and excise duties (Ashwe 1986, p. 28; Awa 1964, p. 194). There was also the perception that the Northern Region received substantially less than it contributed to the central revenue, while the Eastern region received substantially more, and the Western Region slightly less (May 1969, p. 135). Northern political leaders contended that the Eastern Region was being developed at the expense of the Northern Region. They went further, arguing that allocation ought to be made on a per capita basis, whereby the population of a Region would be a determinant factor in its share of central revenue. According to them, the scheme had given the two southern Regions, which had smaller populations, an unfair share of the national revenue, thus, contributing to the Northern Region's backwardness in terms of social development (Awa 1964, p. 32). Of course, any fiscal arrangement predicated upon population was bound to benefit the North because of the Region's numerical strength. Since derivation depended on the tax-paying ability of the people of the Regions, which in turn depended on the wealth of the Regions, it, therefore, follows that the principle would favour the Western Region, since it was the most developed—courtesy of the cocoa boom (Adedeji 1969, pp. 73–74). It should be noted that the period witnessed a boom in the sale of cocoa largely produced in the Western Region. This perception, notwithstanding, the North, and to some extent, the West remained 'surplus' Regions and the East a 'deficit' (Adedeji 1969, p. 62).

Ironically, the same Constitution that sought to promote the unity of the country ended up sowing the seeds of future inter-regional wrangling. The colonial government found itself enmeshed in the political bickering that characterised the Phillipson formula. For instance, the then Governor of Nigeria, Sir Arthur Richards, during a meeting of the Colonial Affairs Study Group of the Empire Parliamentary Association in 1947, posited that:

> I found that the North, which pays its taxes almost as obediently as people do in England, and which contributes more than any other section of Nigeria to the general revenue, is the part of Nigeria which had the least spent on it by the Central Government. The Eastern Provinces, the part of Nigeria which is most vocal and which clamours and calls for more education and for more of everything, is the part which contributes less than the other two regions to the general revenue, and it is also the part upon which the Government has been spending most. (Quoted in Adedeji 1969, p. 63)

Northern leaders seemed to have forgotten that the well-being of one part of the country depended on the well-being of the others and that it was on that foundation that Nigeria was built in the first place. It is pertinent to reiterate that, prior to this period; southern Nigeria was more prosperous than Northern Nigeria because customs duties levied on the trade with both North and South were collected in southern ports. The shortcomings of the Richards' unitary Constitution notwithstanding, the Constitution signalled the birth of fiscal federalism in Nigeria.

Despite the differences among regional elites upon which Region should get what share of the national revenue, delegates during the London Constitutional Conference of 1953, which midwife the Federal Constitution of 1954, were unanimous in their demands for greater regional autonomy in the mould of federalism. This proposal, therefore, made the fiscal adjustment a matter of necessity. Consequently, Sir Louis Chick was appointed Fiscal Commissioner and was required to look into, and report on the financial aspects of the constitutional proposals.[4]

The Fiscal Commissioner began his assignment on a note that the economic development of Nigeria depended upon the fiscal resources of the federal government, and if it was to have the necessary resources to carry out its constitutional responsibilities, its 'reasonable needs' must be interpreted generously and its 'present reserves must not be distributed lavishly to the Regions' (Chick Report 1953, p. 14). Chick maintained that only the revenue collected by the federal government in excess of its own needs would be allocated to the Regions. This implied the acknowledgement that the federal government was in charge of expensive development facilities such as railways, ports, telecommunications, and major roads. It also meant that the federal government would not fail to assist a Regional government that found itself in financial problems. In line with the specific instruction guiding its work, the Chick Commission's recommendations favoured the principle of derivation in that: (i) import, excise and export-duties should be retained by the central government but part of the proceeds reallocated to the Regions on derivation basis; and (ii) the central government should continue to levy personal income-tax, mining royalties, and certain rents and fees for licenses but return the proceeds to the regions according to the residence of tax-payer (Awa 1964, pp. 199–200; May 1969, p. 139).

The implication of these recommendations is that the federal centre became excluded from export taxes, a situation which allowed the Western Region and to some extent the Northern Region to

[4]The Fiscal Commissioner's Report is entitled, 'The Report of the Fiscal Commissioner on the Financial Effects of the Proposed New Constitutional Arrangements (1953) Cmd.9026'. This is hereafter referred to as the *Chick Report, 1953.*

generate substantial amounts from the sale of their commodity products. Meanwhile, the Eastern Region continued to find it difficult to balance its budget. For horizontal allocation, the Commission arrived at the following formula: Northern Region: 30%; Western Region: 40%; Eastern Region: 29%; and Southern Cameroon: 1% (Awa 1964, p. 199). Without a doubt, the emphasis on derivation, once again, deepened the already prevailing economic disparity among the Regions. As usual, political leaders from the North and East expressed their dissatisfaction with the scheme for its excessive reliance on the principle of derivation and continued to demand more revenue for their respective Regions. Eastern Region leaders argued that the decline in revenue from palm produce, which used to be the primary source of the Region's revenue, was the reason behind the East becoming a 'beggar' Region, and it was unfair for the other Regions to ignore this fact (Awa 1964, p. 202). It should be noted that palm produce yields declined as a result of competition in the international market. During this period, the Nigerian economy as a whole depended mainly on the export of primary products, whose prices were subject to fluctuations in the global market. The regional clamour for more revenue is understandable as expansion in regional social services, occasioned by the establishment of a federal system in 1954, had put pressure on Regional budgets.

At the London Constitutional Conference of 1957 where Nigerian delegates discussed Nigeria's independence in 1960, it was decided that a fiscal commission is appointed and mandated to recommend a revenue allocation formula, which would give the Regions the maximum possible measure of independent revenue.[5] Like the one before it, the new Commission headed by Sir Jeremy Raisman and Professor Ronald Tress criticised the prevailing system for placing undue emphasis on derivation, which it argued was based on inaccurate calculations (Raisman Report 1958, p. 50). Despite its criticism of derivation, the Commission recommended that mining rents and royalties were to be allocated 50% to the Region where they were derived, 20% to the federal government, and 30% to the newly established Distributable Pool Account (DPA), for other Regions to share (Raisman Report 1958, p. 25). It would be recalled that under the preceding Chick formula, all revenues from mining rents and royalties went to the Regions of derivation.

[5] Jeremy Raisman and R. C. Tress, Fiscal Commission (1958), hereafter referred to as *The Raisman Report*, 1958.

The Commission went further to propose that the contents of the DPA be distributed thus: 40% for the Northern Region, 24% for the Western Region, 31% for the Eastern Region, and 5% for the Southern Cameroons (Ashwe 1986, p. 32; May 1969, p. 140).

The Raisman fiscal arrangement came into operation in 1959 and was incorporated into the 1960 Independence Constitution. Despite the excitement that greeted independence, elites from both the North and West did not fail to show their disenchantment with the Raisman fiscal arrangement. By this period, the two Regions' financial strength had been weakened because the market in their export commodities had dwindled. Their revenues were not adequate to meet the costs of providing the social services required by their citizens. So, it was not surprising when they began to clamour for a review of the scheme. Conversely, the federal government was experiencing an increase in revenue, thanks to increasing receipts from oil sales. Crude oil was discovered in Nigeria in commercial quantity in 1956. Similarly, the Eastern Region's economic fortunes had also improved due to its newly acquired oil wealth. The federal government became the 'surplus' tier and had to make additional non-statutory transfers to the Regions, which had become fiscally vulnerable.

Despite its economic uplift under this scheme, the Eastern Region too dismissed the Raisman formula as 'extremely unreasonable, unfair and inequitable' (Binns Report 1965, p. 14).[6] This was an indication that the Eastern Region was not satisfied with the 50% allocation from mining rents and royalties it was receiving from the federally-collected revenues. Leaders from the Region particularly sought a full return of revenue from mining rents and royalties. We need to be reminded that the Eastern Region had, before now, favoured revenue allocation on the basis of 'national interest'. The Eastern Region leaders were not unaware that having full access to oil revenue meant huge economic fortunes for their Region. The demand for full return, if granted, would ultimately diminish the financial strength of the federal government.

Regional criticisms made the review of the Raisman scheme almost inevitable but this did not take place until after the introduction of the Republican Constitution of 1963. The review of the scheme became necessary for the following reasons: One, the Southern Cameroons

[6]The Binns Commission Report is hereafter referred to as *Binns Report, 1964*.

ceased to be part of Nigeria in 1961, and its share was divided among the existing Regions; two, the Mid-Western Region was created from the then Western Region in 1963, making Nigeria a federation of four Regions, and the latter's share of the DPA was divided between the newly created unit and the new Western Region. In accordance with Section 164 of the Republican Constitution of 1963, the Binns Commission was appointed in 1964 to review the Raisman formula. In their presentations to the new Commission, political leaders from the Northern Region argued that their Region had been far less able to bridge the gap in its services and investment expenditure than the Eastern Region which had enjoyed more revenue, due to the exploration of oil in that Region (Binns Report 1965, p. 13). The Western Region, now experiencing a dwindling economic fortune, decried the prevailing fiscal arrangement as a 'check' on its rate of economic growth (Binns Report 1965, p. 13). In addition, the Region rejected, in all ramifications, the principle of derivation, which it had supported in the 1950s when it was deriving enormous foreign exchange from the sale of cocoa. Instead, it now supported allocation based on one; population, two; the gap between planned capital expenditure and resources, and three; certain 'objective indicators of minimum responsibility' (May 1969, pp. 141–142).

In its recommendation, the Binns Commission sought to put the principle of derivation on the back-burner, arguing that undue adherence to the principle would weaken the country as a whole. The Commission recommended that 35% of the federally-collected revenue from import duties, mining rents, and royalties be deposited in the DPA and distributed among the Regions as follows: North: 42%; East: 30%; West: 20%; and Mid-West: 8%. According to the Commission, the West's share was increased in order to compensate it for its loss of revenue due to the creation of the Mid-Western Region (in 1963), while the Mid-West's share was increased to provide the newly created Region with enough funds to meet its high cost of administration. Overall, these recommendations greatly benefited the Northern Region, while they benefited the Eastern Region the least and the Western and the Mid-Western Regions only marginally (May 1969, p. 142).

Nevertheless, the 1964 fiscal arrangement, guaranteeing fifty per cent derivation, could not provide any respite for political stability in the country and regional leaders continued to insist on the principle that favoured them the most. Each Region wanted to derive maximum benefits from the resources located within its jurisdiction. This uncompromising attitude reached a high point in 1964 when Eastern Region leaders accused the Northern Region of using its numerical strength in the central government to amass a large proportion of centrally collected revenue. The situation became so heated that the Eastern Region threatened secession (May 1969, p. 143).

Sharing the Oil-Generated Revenue

Sharing of natural resource revenues vary from federation to federation. Nigeria, Russia, and Venezuela are oil-rich federations yet the formula for sharing oil wealth in these countries differs. For example, in Russia, where the federal government has established two petroleum-revenue funds for stabilisation and longer-term saving, most of the producing regions' governments get a 5% share of oil revenues and none of the gas revenues (Anderson 2010, p. 46). The current practice in Nigeria is that oil-producing states get 13% of centrally collected oil revenues from their state in addition to whatever revenues they get from the Federation Account. This is entrenched in the constitution. As Fig. 4.1 illustrates, the derivation principle witnessed a progressive reduction, beginning from 1970 when it was put at 25 to 3% towards the terminal end of military rule.

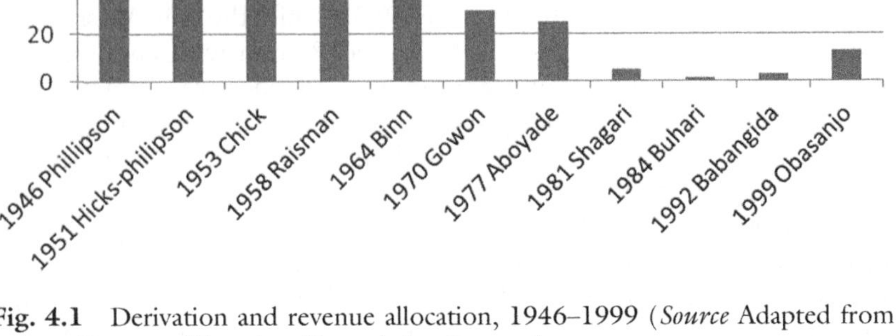

Fig. 4.1 Derivation and revenue allocation, 1946–1999 (*Source* Adapted from various Revenue Allocation Commission Reports)

The practice of sharing oil-generated revenue started during the military era. Nigerian military stormed the country's political stage in January 1966 but there was no attempt at tinkering with the country's fiscal system until during the civil war (1967–1970). The Gowon military government (1966–1975) appointed Chief I. O. Dina in 1969 to chair the 'Interim Revenue Allocation Review Committee.'[7] The Dina Committee proposed a series of principles for sharing the country's centrally-generated revenue, the bulk coming from the sales of crude oil. Once again, the principle of derivation featured. Specifically, the committee recommended that rents and royalties on on-shore oil should be assigned 15% to the federal government, 10% to states on the basis of derivation, 70% to the Special Joint Account (SJA), and 5% to the Special Grants Account (SGA). Revenue from off-shore oil was to be shared 60% to the federal government, 30% to SJA, and 10% to SGA (Elaigwu 2007, p. 224). The implication of this sharing formula is that whatever the states received from the centrally collected revenue, states wherein oil is derived would get an additional share of 10%. Consequently, with the oil-producing states making some gains resulting from the partial application of the derivation principle, the disparity among the states became deepened.

Clearly, the Dina formula favoured the central government as well as the oil-producing states. For example, while the two oil-producing states of Midwest and Rivers received 40.83% of the centrally-generated revenue, the ten other states with 92.7% (51.6 million) of the country's total population, shared among themselves 59.17%. Central revenue was also on the increase because of increased revenues from oil. Expectedly, the Dina Report generated immense debate among the state military governments. For instance, the Western state, which had hitherto favoured derivation, now became an antagonist of the principle.

In spite of the 1999 constitutional provision on the principle of derivation, the newly installed civilian government of Olusegun Obasanjo refused to release the 13% derivation fund due to the oil-producing states from May to December 1999. The bone of contention centred on whether offshore oil was part of the derivation rule or not. The Federal Government believed that offshore oil belonged to the country as a whole, while the oil-producing states claimed that offshore oil should be attributed to the adjoining states and made subject to the derivation

[7]This committee was the first fiscal review body consisting only of Nigerians.

rule (Suberu 2008, p. 462). The Federal Government's interpretation of the derivation rule was heavily criticised. Section 162(2) of the 1999 Constitution was also condemned for creating avenues for complex interpretations in regard to the application of the principle. For instance, the provision fails to specify the location of natural resources, as well as identify the beneficiary of the derivation rule. Ben Nwabueze, a renowned Nigerian legal luminary and a professor of Law, for example, argued that differentiating between onshore and offshore oil for the purpose of the application of the principle of derivation was irrational and aimed at depriving the oil-producing states of their dues (Nwabueze 2007, p. 11).

In order to resolve the impasse around the onshore/offshore dichotomy, the Federal Government had to request the country's apex court to declare that the derivation principle does not apply to offshore oil, and also to seek, among other things, the determination of the seaward boundary of the Oil-producing states. In April 2002, the Supreme Court, in its landmark judgement, reaffirmed the exclusive right of the Federal Government to revenue from offshore oil. This suggests that revenue from offshore oil was not subject to the derivation rule. As expected, the judgement was perceived by the elite in the oil-producing areas as a deliberate ploy by the Federal Government to deprive the oil-producing states of their entitlement and perpetuate a federal fiscal hegemony. However, in the spirit of peace and reconciliation, and perhaps with the April 2003 general elections in sight, President Obasanjo jettisoned the court's pronouncement and adopted a 'political solution' resulting in the enactment of the *Allocation of Revenue (Abolition of Dichotomy in the Application of the Principle of Derivation) Act of 2004*. The Act basically abolishes the dichotomy between resources derived onshore and those derived offshore in the application of the principle of derivation for the purposes of revenue allocation. Thus the Act set aside the Supreme Court's ruling, and derivation was to cover both onshore and offshore oil production. Elites from the Niger Delta, as well as their sympathisers, hailed the enactment of the Act, describing it as a watershed in Nigeria's revenue-sharing practice. However, the non-oil producing states were disenchanted with the political solution. They argued that the Act had unlawfully ceded portions of the country's territorial waters to the oil-producing states, thereby short-changing the non-oil-producing states economically (Suberu 2008, p. 464). They challenged the Act at the Supreme Court but lost. The implementation of the derivation principle has resulted in more oil-generated revenues for the oil-producing states, which have made them richer than their non-oil producing counterparts.

Over-centralisation and Intergovernmental Relations

The journey towards the excessive centralisation of the country's federal system started during the military era. It started effectively on the eve of the civil war (1967–1970) but took root when oil became the economic backbone of the country. The war brought about a number of political and economic measures, which in turn resulted in the federal government assuming a central role, particularly in economic matters. Throughout the war years, the states were subordinated to the centre. The reason for this is simply for effective control of the various divisions of the military. This measure consequently led to the supremacy of the federal government over the states. The central government took over revenue sources previously controlled by the states, thereby leading to a fall in the states' revenues. This was expected as the management of war economy demands some form of unitary control. Writing at the end of the Second World War, Wheare (1963, p. 12) posited that war situations usually produce an increase in the powers of central governments in a federal system and as such, wars and economic crises are enemies of federal government.

The economy of the civil war period, which necessitated a central control, was a significant factor in the centralising trend. But after the war, the centralised command nature of the military continued to impact on the country's practice of federalism. For example, a year after the war, an off-shore oil revenues decree was promulgated giving the federal government exclusive right to off-shore rents and royalties, consequently increasing the financial strength of the centre vis-à-vis the states (Suberu 2001, p. 51). Since a large proportion of federally-collected revenues went to the federal government, state governments had to depend on grants from the central government.

The oil boom of 1973, which coincided with the era of military rule, also increased the economic centrality of the federal government, which in turn contributed to the states' dependence on the federal government. With the federal government enjoying enormous revenue, particularly from oil sales, compared with the states, the centre became the sole distributor of oil rents, dictating which state gets what share of the national oil wealth. This transformed the centre into an arena of competition for access to, and control over oil resources. States, therefore, became extensions of the federal government rather than autonomous tier of government. It is not difficult, therefore, to see how the military transformed Nigeria into an over-centralised federation.

The 1999 Constitution provides that revenues in the Federation Account are to be distributed vertically in the proportions of 48.50, 24, 20 and 7.50% to the federal, states, local governments, and centrally controlled special funds, respectively. A sharing formula that allocates the lion's share of the Federation Account to the federal government, no doubt, ensures federal dominance in fiscal matters. The Constitution provides for two basic legislative lists—the exclusive List with 68 items and concurrent List with 12 items (Constitution of the Federal Republic of Nigeria 1999, pp. 130–138). The former consists of those responsibilities assigned only to the federal government such as currency, defence, foreign policy etc while the latter spells out the responsibilities of both the federal and state governments such as education, health etc. Functions not specified in these lists are assigned to the state governments as residual functions. As Wheare (1963, p. 12) had argued, federalism presupposes that the federal government and the state governments are coordinate and independent, but 'whoever has the residue, neither general nor regional government is subordinate to the other'. With a constitutional arrangement like this, and with the constitutional provision that the federal law prevails in the case of conflict on the concurrent list, it is easy to determine which tier is subordinate to the other.

The centralisation of national revenue has consequently resulted in the 36 states, the Federal Capital Territory, Abuja and the 774 local government areas in Nigeria becoming heavily dependent on the federal centre. In Nigeria, states, being creations of the central government are highly depended on their creator which is increasingly overburdened. This dependency largely impedes the ability of the states to develop their potentials. Not only that, this has, in turn, impacted on the federal-state relations on one the hand and state-local government relations on the other. Of course, federalism presupposes shared-rule but with such issues as primary education, health and local government matters on the concurrent list, conflict is inevitable.

Moreover, the constitutional provision that allows the federal government to interfere in the affairs of the states, no doubt, undermines a state's sovereignty. In Nigeria, the federal government has the power to declare a state of emergency in any state where there is a severe break down of law and order. When this happens, the state governor is suspended and an appointee of the federal government takes charge as administrator. The first time this happened was in 1962 when the Prime Minister, Sir Tafawa Balewa declared a state of emergency on the Western Region. This action was necessitated by the crisis that engulfed the party in power in the Region (the Action Group, AG). Following the declaration, the governor, Chief Samuel L. Akintola and the entire AG-led government were suspended and an interim government, headed by Chief M. A. Majekodunmi was imposed on the Region. The state of emergency lasted for six months. Another leader that exercised this power was President Olusegun Obasanjo when he declared a state of emergency on Plateau state in 2004 as a result of the persistent religious conflict in the state. Similarly, at the beginning of 2012, the Jonathan-led federal government imposed a state of emergency on three of the north-eastern states of Adamawa, Borno and Yobe where Boko Haram's reign of terror was widespread.

One area of federal-state conflict is that of maintenance of law and order at the state level. State governors' inability to maintain security in their states is a common knowledge, especially in the Fourth Republic. For example, as noted earlier, policing falls within the exclusive list but the governor is regarded as the chief security officer of the state. Ironically, the governor is not in charge of the police force, the president is. Nigerians have been fed with stories of situations where state commissioners of police ignored orders from governors on the ground that they were only answerable to the Inspector-General of Police, who is in turn, answerable to the president.

Analysis of federal-state relations in the Fourth Republic will not be complete without making reference to the frosty relationship between the federal government and Lagos state under Olusegun Obasanjo and Bola Tinubu respectively. The creation of new local government councils by the Governor in 2004 set the state on a collision with the federal government. President Obasanjo argued that the act was a breach of the country's constitution, and went on to deprive Lagos state of its allocation of the Federation Account. The country's Senate sided with the president, arguing that the action violated Section 8(3) of the Constitution, which provides that the creation of new local governments should be subjected to a referendum.[8] Lagos state had to take the federal

[8]For details of cases where President Olusegun Obasanjo undermined the autonomy of state governments, see Elaigwu (2002, pp. 79–83) and Warisu (2016, p. 105).

government to court. Interestingly, the Supreme Court gave judgment in favour of Lagos state and ordered the federal government to release the funds in question. The Court ruled that the federal government had illegally withheld Lagos state's funds but the Presidency disobeyed the ruling. Lagos state was denied its dues till the end of Obasanjo's tenure in 2007. Reference has also been made to how Obasanjo refused to respect the constitutional provision in regards to the derivation principle in 2002, and this does not need rehashing here.

Likewise, state-local government relationship is also characterised by cases of undue interference in local government affairs from state governors. Local government councils are supposed to be autonomous of state governments but in practice, they are subordinate to the state governments that created them. They are constitutionally allowed to provide such services that benefit the grassroots population, and these include primary and secondary education, refuse disposal, registration of births and deaths. However, these internally generated revenue sources are usually inadequate to match their constitutional responsibilities, hence their reliance on the Federation Account that comes through the state governments. As if it is a rule, a recalcitrant chairman is usually 'punished' by withholding statutory allocations meant for that local government. These reasons partly explain why the local governments lack autonomy.

Federal-state relations, however, witnessed some form of cooperation in 2015 when President Muhammadu Buhari released some bailout funds to about 30 out of 36 state governments to help fill their fiscal gap. These states' financial glitch was so acute that they could not pay salaries of civil servants.

It is important to return to our definition of federalism as a system in which governmental powers are divided between the general and regional governments in a co-ordinate and independent manner. This implies that each tier has an independent role to play in the federation but states in Nigeria are at a disadvantaged position, due to their subordinate nature. This has largely given rise to the clamour for restructuring and true federalism.

Conclusion

Revenue allocation is the most contentious aspect of Nigeria's federal system. As we have seen, the 1946 and 1951 fiscal schemes allowed source federating units to obtain 50% of revenue derived from their territories, whilst the 1953 scheme provided for 100%. It would be recalled that the governments of the Northern and Western Regions favoured the principle of derivation when groundnuts and cocoa were the major sources of revenue for these two Regions respectively. They only opposed this sharing formula when oil was found in the Eastern Region. As shown in the chapter, no single fiscal scheme escaped criticisms from regional political leaders. Each time a new scheme was introduced some federating units benefited while others lost out. It has been very difficult for the leaders to find an acceptable formula for both horizontal and vertical sharing arrangements. Each federating unit seeks maximum benefits from the system. There is no denying that regional wealth inequality has contributed to differing needs, and has particularly been responsible for the inter-regional conflicts dominating the country's revenue sharing practice. Clearly, the manner in which assignment of taxes is done in federations makes constituent units unlikely to be able to raise sufficient revenue from independent sources to match their expenditure. As we have seen, the centre controls the most lucrative sources of revenue while the federating units are left with the less lucrative sources. This fiscal arrangement exacerbates the economic disparity that exists among the states. However, politics, more than economics, no doubt, plays a significant role in shaping the revenue allocation system.

Nigeria's political leaders have, at every phase of the country's political history made significant efforts to achieve efficient and equitable sharing of revenue between the different tiers of governments. However, as laudable as the objectives of the fiscal principles adopted are, they have proved to be unworkable. One problem with these principles is that they are in conflict with one another. Therefore, relying solely on any of them brings problem and applying them simultaneously does not solve the problem. The principle of derivation, for example, works at cross purpose with that of need. The principle exacerbates regional inequality as the rich states get richer and the poor ones get poorer. However, one major advantage of derivation is that it brings about healthy competition among the states as those not so endowed with natural resources devises other means to generate revenue from within. It is obvious that the fundamental problem with revenue sharing in Nigeria is the near absolute concentration of resources at the centre. This has given rise to the over-politicisation of the system that creates animosity and perpetual disagreements among the parties involved.

References

Adedeji, A. (1969). *Nigerian Federal Finance: Its Development, Problems and Prospects*. London: Hutchinson

Aiyede, R. (2009, June). The Political Economy of Fiscal Federalism and the Dilemma of Constructing a Developmental State in Nigeria. *International Political Science Review, 30*(3), 249–269.

Anderson, A. (2010). *Fiscal Federalism: A Comparative Introduction*. Oxford: Oxford University Press.

Ashwe, C. (1986). *Fiscal Federalism in Nigeria* (Research Monograph No. 46). Canberra: Centre for Research on Federal Financial Relations, Australian National University.

Awa, E. (1964). *Federal Government in Nigeria*. Berkeley and Los Angeles: University of California Press.

Awa, E. (1976). *Issues in Federalism*. Benin City: Ethiope Publishing Corporation.

Boadway, R., & Shah, A. (2009). *Fiscal Federalism: Principles and Practice of Multiorder Governance*. Cambridge: Cambridge University Press.

Burgess, M. (2006). *Comparative Federalism: Theory and Practice*. London and New York: Routledge.

Danjuma, T. Y. (1996). Revenue Sharing and the Political Economy of Nigerian Federalism. In J. Elaigwu & R. A. Akindele (Eds.), *Federalism and Nation Building in Nigeria: The Challenges of the 21st Century*. Abuja: Nigerian Journal of Inter-Governmental Relations.

Ekpo, A. (2006). Federal Republic of Nigeria. In A. Shah (Ed.), *The Practice of Fiscal Federalism: Comparative Perspectives* (A Global Dialogue on Federalism), Vol. 4. Montreal: McGill-Queen's University Press.

Elaigwu, J. (2002). Federalism in Nigeria's New Democratic Polity. *Publius: The Journal of Federalism, 32*(2), 79–83.

Elaigwu, J. (2007). *The Politics of Federalism in Nigeria*. London: Adonis & Abbey Publishers.

FGN. (1999). *Constitution of the Federal Republic of Nigeria*. Lagos: Federal Government Press.

Freinkman, L. (2008). Intergovernmental Relations in Nigeria: Improving Service Delivery in Core Sectors. In J. Elaigwu (Ed.), *Fiscal Federalism in Nigeria: Facing the Challenges of the Future*. London: Adonis & Abbey Publishers.

Galadima, H. (2008). Division of Powers and Responsibilities (Including Tax Powers) in Nigeria. In J. Elaigwu (Ed.), *Fiscal Federalism in Nigeria: Facing the Challenges of the Future*. London: Adonis & Abbey Publishers.

Iyoha, M. (2008). Fiscal Federalism: Towards Coping with and Resolving Future Challenges. In J. Elaigwu (Ed.), *Fiscal Federalism in Nigeria: Facing the Challenges of the Future*. London: Adonis & Abbey Publishers.

Maddox, W. (1941, December). The Political Basis of Federation. *The American Political Science Review, 35*(6), 1120–1127.

May, J. (1969). *Federalism and Fiscal Adjustment*. Oxford: Clarendon Press.

Nigeria. (1953). *Report of the Fiscal Commissioner on the Financial Effects of the Proposed New Constitutional Arrangements, Cmd.9026*. Report by Louis Chick. Lagos: Government Printers.

Nigeria. (1958). *Preliminary Report of the Fiscal Commission*. Report by J. Raisman & Trees. Lagos: Government Printers.

Nigeria. (1965). *Fiscal Review Commission*. Report by K. J. Binns. Lagos: Government Printers.

Nwabueze, B. (2007). *How President Obasanjo Subverted Nigeria's Federal System*. Ibadan, Abuja, and Owerri: Gold Press Limited.

Oates, W. (1972). *Fiscal Federalism*. New York: Harcourt Brace Jovanorich.

Oates, W. (1999). An Essay on Fiscal Federalism. *Journal of Economic Literature, XXXVII*(9), 1120–1149.

Olaloku, A. F. (1979). Nigerian Federal Finance: Issues and Choices. In A. B. Akinyemi, et al. (Eds.), *Readings on Federalism*. Lagos, Nigeria: The Nigerian Institute of International Affairs (NIIA).

Oyediran, O., & Olagunju, O. (1979). The Military and the Politics of Revenue Allocation. In O. Oyediran (Ed.), *Nigerian Government and Politics Under Military Rule 1966–79*. London and Basingstoke: Macmillan.

Phillips, A. (1971). Nigeria's Federal Fiscal Experience. *The Journal of Modern African Studies, 9*(3), 398–408.

Phillips, A. (1991). Managing Fiscal Federalism: Revenue Allocation Issues. *Publius: The Journal of Federalism, 21*, 103–111.

Suberu, R. (2001). *Federalism and Ethnic Conflict in Nigeria*. Washington, DC: United States Institute of Peace Press.

Suberu, R. (2008). The Supreme Court and Federalism in Nigeria. *Journal of Modern African Studies, 46*(3), 451–485.

Vile, M. J. C. (1961). *The Structure of American Federalism*. Oxford: Oxford University Press.

Warisu, A. (2016). Federal-State Relations in Nigerian Federalism. In O. Ibeanu & M. J. Kuna (Eds.), *Nigerian Federalism: Continuing Quest for Stability and Nation-Building*. Ibadan: Safari Books.

Watts, R. (1966). *New Federations: Experiments in the Commonwealth*. Oxford: Clarendon Press.

Watts, R. (1999). *Comparing Federal Systems* (2nd ed.). Montreal and Kingston: McGill-Queen's University Press.
Watts, R. (2003). Introduction: Comparative Research and Fiscal Federalism. *Regional and Federal Studies, 13*(4), 1–6.
Wheare, K. (1963). *Federal Government* (4th ed.). London: Oxford University Press.

CHAPTER 5

Secession and Self-Determination in Nigeria

Introduction

As shown in previous chapters, the unequal distribution of national wealth, especially oil-generated revenue, drives conflicts in the oil-rich federation. This is why scholars such as Collier (2008) describe resource wealth as a problem (p. 39); as messing up politics (p. 44); and as a trap (p. 50). Any of these phrases or a combination of them may be used to explain the negative impact of oil rents on Nigerian politics and economy and the federal system in particular. Irrespective of how it is viewed, the fear of domination of one group by the other is an integral part of Nigerian politics. It has contributed to the series of threat of secession and the seemingly unending agitation for self-determination in the country.

The chapter starts with the discussion of the meaning of secession, especially in relation to federations, as well as the politics of secession in Nigeria. Scholars have, in different degrees, addressed the question of secession in federations, as well as in unitary states. We are, however, interested in the relationship between secession and federation. We also discuss an actual attempt by the defunct Eastern Region, populated mainly by the Igbo ethnic group to secede. The 'fear factor' cannot be ruled out in the civil war (1967–1970) that rocked the country just six years after independence. Discussing the civil war is an attempt to buttress the argument that distributing both political and economic

D. Babalola, *The Political Economy of Federalism in Nigeria*, Federalism and Internal Conflicts,
https://doi.org/10.1007/978-3-030-05493-9_5

resources in Nigeria has never been rancour-free and has given rise to political instability.

In addition, the chapter also discusses the various dimensions of agitations by ethnic minority groups in the Niger Delta region for self-determination. These agitations have resulted from the fear of marginalisation in the distribution of the country's oil-generated wealth. Elites from the oil-producing states of the Niger Delta have continuously mounted a vociferous challenge against the revenue sharing formula. They have, particularly, decried the near abandonment of the principle of derivation, which they claim is inimical to their interest. Another significant development immediately following the re-establishment of civilian rule in 1999 was the Sharia issue, which developed into a major political confrontation between twelve northern state governments and the Federal Government. The adoption of the Islamic legal system may be perceived as an attempt to seek self-determination as a result of the feelings of marginalisation harboured by the northern elite in the new political dispensation.

Secession and Self-Determination in Federations

Secession, as relates to federalism, may be defined as the pulling out or the withdrawal of a territory and its inhabitants from an existing sovereign federal state. It is about breaking up an existing federal state. Secession is usually orchestrated by a geographically concentrated minority (sometimes, majority) group. The aim of secession is usually to create a sovereign territorial entity. Secession is usually predicated upon a number of justifications.

First, more often than not, the desire for secession is rooted in the deprivation of basic rights. According to Buchanan (1991, 1995), secession may be justified if a group or a region in the federation suffers serious injustices at the hands of the state or if a group suffers oppression from people of other ethnic groups(s). The region may have a reason to break away if the national government had continuously failed to protect the rights of the citizens of the region. In all of this, as argued by Birch (1989, p. 64), 'temporary grievances' are not enough to justify secession; they must have history and 'be likely to persist indefinitely'.

Second, another ground for justification is marginalisation. An ethnic group, especially when geographically concentrated in one area may consider pulling out of an existing state if it feels marginalised politically and/or economically. Ethnic rivalries and tensions, for example, contributed to the emergence of secessionist movements in Biafra (Nigeria), Catalonia (Spain) and Quebec (Canada).

Third, secession may also be justified if the federal bargain has been undermined to the extent that it has failed to satisfy the goals of one or more parts of the federation, or if the federation has somehow become less federal in its nature and operation (Burgess 2006, pp. 280–281). What this implies is that a part of the federation may consider quitting the union if it loses interest in the union. This was the claim of the political elite in the defunct Eastern Region in the build-up to the civil war.

Fourth, another justifying condition is if a part of the union was forced into the union, especially when 'its people had displayed a continuing refusal to give full consent to the union' (Birch 1989, p. 64). The framers of the Ethiopian Constitution of 1995, for example, inserted the secession clause in the Constitution, perhaps because of their recognition that a part or more may decide to opt out of the imposed union in the future. Although it has been argued that as symbolic as the clause is, it is unlikely that any of the federating units in the multi-ethnic federation would be allowed to secede (Habtu 2005). This is where the nexus between the origin and success or failure of a federation becomes useful.

Given that every federation is characterised by a myriad of centrifugal forces, one may be compelled to align with Ayoade's (1973, p. 63) postulation that federations are prone to secession. Some scholars, however, hold divergent views, arguing that secession is not compatible with federalism. Edward Freeman is in this category as he argued that a federation was 'essentially a perpetual union because it is inconceivable for a federal constitution to contain provisions for its own dissolution' (cited in Burgess 2006, p. 271). This is suggesting that once the 'offer' and 'acceptance' for a federal union is concluded the federal bargain or 'contract' is binding and any attempt by any of the parties, be it a constituent unit or the general government to breach the contract was an act of rebellion. The crux of the argument here is that secession is a rebellion and has no place in a federal constitution.

K. C. Wheare (1963), drawing from his observation of the federations of Australia, Canada, Switzerland and the United States concurred that the constituent units in these federations had no right to secede and the federal government had no right to expel any unit. He, however, argued that the non-inclusion of the secession clause in the constitutions of these countries does not mean that secession was inconsistent with federalism (1963, pp. 86–87). The point being made here is that, though, secession is compatible with federalism but is antithetical to good federal government. This explains why governments deploy their instruments of coercion to resist secession. Attempts to secede usually lead to civil war such as the one experienced in Nigeria when the defunct state of Biafra seceded from Nigeria in 1967.

Similarly, having observed that the British-inspired federations of India, Malaysia, Nigeria and Pakistan made no provision for secession, Watts (1966, pp. 309–310) advanced the following three arguments against secession in a federation: (i) fear of subordination that endangers the principle of co-ordinate governments; (ii) weakening of the federal system because it gives a 'weapon of political coercion' to the regional governments; and (iii) possibility of disintegration may frustrate nation-building and national development. For Watts, therefore, not tolerating secession in these federations was a wise move because inserting secession clause in their constitutions would have negatively impacted on the process of nation-building. In his own contribution to the debate over the relationship between secession and federalism, King (1982) argued that there is no legal provision preventing federating units from seceding but secession move is in conflict with the federal government's constitutional duty towards the citizens in the seceding unit. For King, the structure of federal governments is heavily weighted against secession (p. 109).

On the other side of the debate was Dikshit (1975). Relying on the American Declaration of Independence of 1776, he argued that when a territorial group finds it impossible to coexist with another group within the union, that group may decide to 'dissolve the political bonds which have connected them with another…' (p. 68). In other words, secession may be justified if the federation's terms of reference have been breached either in part or wholly.

Let us bring this debate to a close by agreeing with Burgess (2006, p. 276) that secession may be 'theoretically inconsistent with federation but probably desirable in practice'. Practically, it is not illegal and may be desirous, especially in a federation where a party to the union does not feel a sense of belonging. If we accept that a federation is a voluntary union, then secession should be consistent with federalism. Even an imposed federation such as Ethiopia recognises that separation might become expedient in the future. But why secede? The goal of secession is self-determination.

Self-Determination

Unlike secession, self-determination is not about breaking up an existing sovereign federal state. Rather, it is concerned with the right of a people to decide their own political status. It may give rise to a separate state but this is usually not the aim. The demand for self-determination may be aimed at the state's recognition of a group's culture and language. It basically means political autonomy, which is the right to possess powers of legislation, administration and adjudication in specific areas. Thus, self-determination, or what Lapidoth (1997, p. 33) refers to as 'territorial political autonomy', is a political arrangement aimed at granting to a group the right to express its distinct identity. The term is, more often than not, used to describe the right of peoples under colonial rule or foreign domination, to control their affairs as they desire and not necessarily 'internal national minorities' (Kymlicka 1995, p. 27).

The United Nations' Charter, for example, provides that, 'all peoples have the right to self-determination'. Similarly, the Declaration on the Rights of Indigenous Peoples also endorses the principle of self-determination for indigenous peoples. It is important to point out that both the Charter and the Declaration appear to be silent on the definition of 'peoples'. However, they both show that self-determination is concerned with rectifying historic injustice. Self-determination is about internal autonomy and may be relevant for minorities who suffer historical discrimination in the existing federal union. Scholars are of the view that like in the case of secession, national minorities might have a claim of self-determination if membership of a federal union was involuntary (Danley 1991 cited in Kymlicka 1995, p. 117).

In the Nigerian context, self-determination means the right by an ethnic group or a federating unit to manage its political and economic affairs. As argued by Osaghae (2003, p. 85), self-determination is a political weapon usually employed by aggrieved and redress-seeking groups such as those in the Niger Delta, in their struggle for what they perceive to be just and equitable political arrangements. For the people of the Niger Delta, where the bulk of Nigeria's oil is derived, controlling own resources—fiscal autonomy—is a solution to political marginalisation and majority ethnic domination, and a strategy of political accommodation in the multi-ethnic Nigerian federal state. Their struggle for self-determination, therefore, is a fight against ethnic majority domination or put differently, political marginalisation; it is about political and economic autonomy and institutional integration. Political leaders in this part of the country are particularly concerned with how the resources found within their jurisdiction would benefit people in the area, clearly explaining why they are agents of self-determination and not agents of secession.

Fear of Domination and the Politics of Secession

As explained earlier, the multiplicity inherent in the Nigerian federation makes the call for secession almost inevitable. In Nigeria, each ethnic group lives in fear of being marginalised in the scheme of things. For instance, the educationally advantaged Yoruba and Igbo ethnic groups often express the fear that the educationally disadvantaged but more populous Hausa-Fulani ethnic group would use their numeric advantage to out-compete other groups in the struggle for national resources. In the same token, the Hausa-Fulani ethnic group has always been fearful that the other two major groups may use their educational advantage to dominate the other members of the federal union. For example, in an attempt to address the fear of domination hovering over the Northern Region, its leaders introduced the famous policy of Northernisation in 1955. This meant that in the Northern civil service, preference would be given to appointing a Northern Nigerian, but, where no Northern Nigerian was available with the requisite qualifications, a contract appointment of a European would be preferred to the permanent recruitment of a Nigerian from the South (Kirk-Greene 1967, p. 8). Expectedly, the reception of this policy was bitter in the South. Likewise, the minorities live in perpetual fear of domination. As observed by Kirk-Greene,

> fear has been constant in every tension and confrontation in political Nigeria. Not the physical fear of violence, not the spiritual fear of retribution, but the psychological fear of discrimination, of domination. It is the fear of not getting one's fair share, one's dessert. (1975, p. 19)

The fear factor has also been partly responsible for the series of secession threat in Nigeria. Secession is a recurrent threat in Nigeria's political lexicon dating back to 1951 (this was before the adoption of a federal political framework). That year, the Northern Region, fearing a southern domination, demanded fifty percent representation in the central legislature, and insisted that if this was not granted, the Region would secede (Ayoade 1973, p. 65). This threat yielded some fruits as the region's demand was granted. Similarly, as pointed out in Chapter 2, the North threatened to secede in early 1953 because the Region did not want to be rushed into self-rule. The reason behind the North's lack of readiness was nothing but its fear of southern domination in a self-governing Nigeria. Also in the same year, the Western Region threatened to secede if Lagos was separated from the Region. As suggested by Ayoade (1973, p. 67), the feeling of self-sufficiency on the part of the Region partly accounted for the threat. Although the Yoruba elite lost out in their attempt to break away in 1953, the issue of secession remained strong in their minds. Therefore, during the 1954 constitutional conference held in Lagos, they sought to have the right of secession inserted in the proposed federal constitution but they failed in this attempt as the emergent Constitution did not include the right to secede.

Not having a secession clause in the Federal Constitution did not stop the Eastern Region from threatening to secede from the federation over the perceived manipulated general elections held in 1964, as well as over the 1964 fiscal scheme, which guaranteed fifty percent derivation. The Region was not satisfied with the fiscal arrangement as it wanted a hundred percent derivation. Consequently, the Region saw no point in remaining in a federal union in which it makes huge financial contribution to national revenue but was not able to exercise a corresponding political power. This again reinforces the view that oil was part of the story of the civil war.

The Northern Region also made a similar threat in mid-1966 as a result of that year's coup, which claimed the lives of notable northern political and military leaders. Unlike the January coup, which was aimed at seizing power, the orchestrated counter-coup of July of that year was aimed at secession. Many Northerners, already incensed by the killings of their leaders wanted *araba* (secession) (Ademoyega 1981, pp. 120–122).

The Civil War (1967–1970)

Secession threat used to be seen as a weapon of redress by ethno-regional groups in the country. This changed, however, in May 1967 when the then Eastern Region military governor, Colonel Odumegwu Ojukwu, proclaimed the Republic of Biafra. Consequently, 'negotiable secession' became 'actual secession'. Gowon responded to Ojukwu's pronouncement by reiterating the federal government's resolve to prevent secession, thereby setting the stage for a war.

Scholars and commentators on Nigerian politics have offered different views on the causes of the civil war. Caution, must, however, be exercised when dissecting these views because people have given accounts of the war depending on which side they belong(ed) or have sympathy for. Nonetheless, reasons for the war could be found in the events that preceded the war, including, but not limited to the first two military coup d'états that occurred in 1966. Nigeria experienced its first military coup in January 1966 when some young army officers, mainly from the Eastern Region overthrew the first civilian government, which was accused of corruption among other things. At the time of the coup, the civilian government had lost control of the governance of the country. Corruption, nepotism, and unhealthy competition for national resources had become a culture in the country.

As expected in a multi-ethnic society like Nigeria, there were mixed reactions to the coup in which the country's Prime Minister, Sir Tafawa Balewa (Fulani), the Northern Region Premier, Sir Ahmadu Bello (Fulani), the Premier of Western Region, Chief Samuel Akintola (Yoruba), and the Federal Commissioner of Finance, Chief Festus Okotie-Eboh (Itsekiri, Mid-Western Region) were assassinated. As far as the Northern elite were concerned, the coup was ethnically inspired to eliminate them from the country's power equation. Their argument was predicated on the fact that the coup was led by Igbo soldiers and the major victims were from the North. Although, one of the surviving major actors in the coup, a Yoruba army officer, Adewale Ademoyega, denies ethnic considerations in the execution of the coup but the northern elite would prefer to argue otherwise. The coup was, nonetheless, welcomed and celebrated in the Western Region where it was believed that politicians' lust for power and unhealthy competition of national resources had plunged the Region, and indeed the country into a serious political crisis. People in this Region had hoped that military rule would bring about some semblance of sanity in the polity. It must be stressed that this coup played a part in sowing the seeds for a future crisis in the country.

Major-General Johnson Aguiyi-Ironsi, an Igbo, being the most senior army officer in the country upstaged the original coup plotters and became the first military Head of State to rule Nigeria. Some of the steps taken by Ironsi further deepened the ethnic division in the country, as well as the fear of domination. For example, he promulgated the Unification Decree No. 34, which abolished Nigeria's federal system replacing it with a unitary system. The decree also unified the civil services thereby undermining the Northernisation policy (Anber 1967, p. 163). This particular move seemed to confirm the fear of the Northern elite that the Igbo ethnic group wanted to dominate other ethnic groups and particularly deprive them of power in a federal Nigeria. Moreover, the statistics of the January coup were not lost on the Northern political elite, who allegedly mobilised their followers to disown the new military government as well as to protest against Decree No. 34 (Panter-Brick 1970, p. 24). This resulted in a series of anti-Igbo riots in some major northern cities like Kano and Kaduna in which many Igbos were killed. It was in the midst of this uproar that the July counter-coup took place. It may be argued that transforming Nigeria into a unitary state was perhaps aimed at resolving inter-ethnic and other regional conflicts. However, the Nigerian military which had itself become ethnicised lacked the capacity and integrity to handle such restructuring. The Nigerianisation of the army, a by-product of the nation-building process, which began in 1958, gave rise to its politicisation. Moreover, the introduction of a quota system in recruitment and promotion in 1962 deepened the politicisation (Gutteridge 1969, pp. 63–64). Theoretically, the quota system was to ensure that all the geopolitical regions in the country produced equal numbers of people for recruitment and promotion. In reality, however, the system did not give room for selection and promotion based on merit as politicians encouraged people from their regions or ethnic groups to enlist in the military. This development marked the beginning of the ethnicisation of the military. With the Nigerian army now controlled by Nigerian politicians, nepotism, a feature of Nigerian politics crept into recruitment and promotion exercises.

The July 1966 counter-coup was executed mainly by Northern army officers, and casualties were mainly from the East, giving rise to the thinking that the coup was a revenge by the Northerners. The counter-coup further deepened the polarisation of the army along ethnic lines, especially when the then Lieutenant-Colonel Yakubu Gowon became the next Head of State. Gowon's first step was to restore the federal system of government, a move not acceptable to the Eastern Region Governor, Colonel Odumegwu Ojukwu and the Igbo elite who feared that the Federal Government would soon assume a position where it would be able to overawe the states. Not only that, Ojukwu also objected to Gowon's accession to the office of Head of State on the ground that Gowon was not the most senior military officer in the Nigerian army but Brigadier Babafemi Ogundipe, a Yoruba officer and the Chief of Staff, Supreme Headquarters. Ogundipe was the de facto second in command to Ironsi but fled the country when some junior military officers from the north refused to accept his authority (Ademoyega 1981, p. 125). The face-off between these two army officers, combined with other factors culminated in the civil war. In May 1967, Ojukwu proclaimed that the territory and region known as Eastern Nigeria together with her continental shelf and territorial water shall henceforward be an independent sovereign state of the name and title of 'The Republic of Biafra' (Kirk-Greene 1970, pp. 451–452). Clearly, for Ojukwu, territorial secession was the solution to the interethnic hostility that saw his fellow Igbos massacred in large number in the North in mid-1966.

The war may be described as a manifestation of the ethno-regional politics that had become a feature of the Nigerian army in particular and that of Nigerian politics in general. That is, a manifestation of a crisis of hegemony between the Northern elite and their counterparts in the East. For the Northern elite, the January coup was aimed at diminishing their political power in the country, and for their counterparts in the East, the counter-coup of July 1966 meant a loss of political and economic power to the Igbo ethnic group.

Another factor contributing to the war was how to resolve the grey areas in the prevailing federal structure. Gowon wanted what he had referred to as a 'tight federation' in which there would be a strong centre. This was presumably an attempt to avoid the mistakes of the first experiment at federalism where the federating units were more powerful than the centre. Meanwhile, Ojukwu wanted a system in the mould of confederalism; a system that would enable the constituent units to have absolute control over its resources, notably oil (Panter-Brick 1970, pp. 29–31). Ojukwu did not hide his disapproval for the practice of Nigerian federalism. In a statement in 1969 while the war was still ongoing, he said:

> … the Nigerian Federation in the form it was constituted by the British cannot by any stretch of imagination be considered an African necessity. Yet we are being forced to sacrifice our very existence as a people to the

integrity of that ramshackle creation that has no justification either in history or in the freely expressed wishes of the people. (Ojukwu 1969, pp. 18–19)

In light of the central argument underpinning this book, going beyond the prevalent argument centred on the fear of domination thesis, the civil war might also be viewed as a struggle for the protection of great economic resources—oil. Some commentators are of the view that the fact that Nigeria will be a great oil producer in the not too distant future was 'one of the root causes of the crisis' (Armstrong 1967, p. 5). Others have argued that oil wealth may not necessarily be the main cause of the war but a contributing factor, because oil held out the prospect of a solid economic base, especially to the Eastern Region where most of Nigeria's oil was produced. It could be argued that the Igbo elite perceived secession as an opportunity to control the oil wealth, and it is equally credible to argue that the fear of losing the same oil wealth contributed to the federal government's determination to prevent secession. Also, with the fast-declining revenues from agriculture, northern and western politicians would, expectedly, not be in favour of secession. Elites from both Regions were aware of the potential political and economic gains derivable from oil wealth.

Oil-Producing Minority Groups and the Agitation for Self-Determination

Nigeria's major economic resource (oil) is located mainly in the Niger Delta area inhabiting over twenty different ethnic groups, including those of Anang, Bini, Efik, Ibibio, Igbo, Ijaw, Itsekiri, Ogba, Ogoni, Ukwuani, Urhobo and Yoruba, with the Ijaw constituting the largest (Dike 1956, p. 25). Geographically, the Niger Delta is situated in the central part of Southern Nigeria or the South-South geopolitical zone.[1] The entire area is made up of six states, namely, Akwa Ibom, Bayelsa,

[1] During the Sani Abacha military era (1993–1998), Nigeria was divided into six geopolitical zones, namely, North Central (Benue, Kogi, Kwara, Nasarawa, Niger and Plateau states), North-East (Adamawa, Bauchi, Borno, Gombe, Taraba and Yobe states), North-West (Jigawa, Kaduna, Kano, Katsina, Kebbi, Sokoto and Zamfara states), South-West (Ekiti, Lagos, Ogun, Ondo, Osun and Oyo states), South-East (Abia, Anambra, Ebonyi, Enugu, and Imo states) and South-South (Akwa Ibom, Bayelsa, Cross River, Delta, Edo and Rivers).

Cross River, Delta, Edo and Rivers. These states, together with Abia and Imo in the South-East and Ondo in the South-West constitute the main oil-producing states in Nigeria.

The oil-producing minority groups' demand for self-determination, is, as far as they are concerned, predicated on their economic status as 'producers' of the country's wealth. Their continuous quest for self-determination within the context of the multi-ethnic federation is a political demand, which they believe if granted, would guarantee them control over the resources found in their domain. They persistently demand their own exclusive political and economic space using the euphemism of 'resource control'. In the Nigerian context, the term means a resource sharing practice that allows states of the federation to have control over the natural resources within their territories and make contributions to the central government to fund federal responsibilities. This demand is about breaking the monopoly of federal control over oil resource, as well as is a solution to political marginalisation and majority ethnic domination.

The clamour for self-determination by the people of the Niger Delta has a long history and has taken different forms. This initially took the form of a demand for separate constituent units, a demand that was not granted by the Willinks Commission of 1958, and a demand for an independent state, such as the one declared by Isaac Boro in 1966. The struggle then shifted back to demands for separate constituent units that would enhance the agitators' access to political participation in the affairs of the Nigerian state and ultimately control over the resources within the jurisdiction. The shift in emphasis was occasioned by the events that trailed the civil war. The minorities of the Niger Delta had hoped that the state creation exercise that preceded the civil war would allow them political participation as well as economic benefits from the centre. However, these hopes were dashed and even became far-fetched with a shift from the principle of derivation to those of equality and population of states, which benefited the major ethnic groups that had historically marginalised the minorities (Obi 1998, p. 269).

As independence became imminent, the cry by the ethnic minorities for self-determination became louder, giving rise to the setting up of the Sir Henry Willink's Commission of 1958. Specifically, the Commission was to inquire into the fears of the minority groups that the prevailing political structure had the tendency to result in the domination of the minorities by the majority groups in the then three Regions of the federation. With specific reference to the minorities in the Niger Delta, the Commission refused to yield to the pressure to recommend the creation of separate constituent units and reasoned that creating new constituent units would not solve the minority problem. It had hoped that following independence in 1960, there would be a shift of political gravity from the regions to the centre and this would encourage inter-ethnic and inter-regional alliances that would allay the fears of the minorities (Osaghae 2003, p. 93). Having noted that the Niger Delta area was poor, backward and neglected, the Commission recommended the creation of a special development agency to address the developmental problems of the Niger Delta area and this informed the establishment of the Niger Delta Development Board (NDDB) in 1960. Although the Commission failed to recommend the creation of separate constituent units for the minorities, the establishment of this Commission was the first attempt by the Nigerian state to pay attention to the minority question.

The quest for self-determination continued after independence when the late Isaac Jasper Adaka Boro, who had protested the administrative neglect suffered by the oil-producing area, declared the ill-fated Republic of Niger Delta in 1966. Boro, who hailed from Kaiama town in present Bayelsa state left the university to lead an armed struggle against the federal government which was accused of marginalising the area producing the wealth of the nation. Boro's attempted secession was aimed at ensuring that the Niger Delta region controlled its affairs, as well as its resources. The 'revolution' lasted for twelve days before it was brutally suppressed by the Nigerian state which sentenced Boro and his men to death but was later pardoned. Boro failed in his quest for an independent state, but his agitation set a precedent for the struggle for self-determination in the oil-rich region.

Another notable ethnic movement that sprang up in the early 1990s in the Niger Delta area was the Movement for the Survival of the Ogoni People (MOSOP). MOSOP was formed and led by the late Ken Saro Wiwa ostensibly to articulate the demand of the Ogoni people for self-determination within the Nigerian federation. Having complained for decades regarding the environmental degradation caused by oil exploitation in the region as well as a lack of access to political, economic and social opportunities in terms of infrastructural development, the Ogoni people, using the platform of MOSOP, presented the famous *Ogoni Bill of Rights* (OBR) to the Federal Military Government

(FMG) of Nigeria and the Nigerian people in 1990. The Bill specifically demanded that the Ogoni people be granted political autonomy allowing them the control of the economic resources found in Ogoniland for Ogoni development (*Ogoni Bill of Rights* 1990, p. 11; also in Naanen [1995, p. 67]; Obi [2006, p. 25]). Ogoniland has been described as 'a socio-economic paradox' because it is the 'poorest and most industrialised enclave in Nigeria' (Naanen 1995, p. 66). Ogoni people believe that the area is the food basket of the country yet the poorest. This assertion has, however, been debunked, with Osaghae (1995) noting that the Ogonis have benefitted more than other minorities in appointments to top government positions, which are usually the yardstick for measuring access to state power in Nigeria.[2] Nonetheless, the Ogoni demands were predicated on the claim that the Ogoni people have contributed in no small measure to the economy of Nigeria and as such deserved better.

As argued by Osaghae (2003, p. 98), by demanding self-determination for Nigerian ethnic communities, the Ogoni Bill implied a loss of faith in the ability of the Nigerian state, as controlled by the majority ethnic groups, to protect the interests of minorities. Ogoni people believed that their predicament was as a result of their political and economic powerlessness in the multi-ethnic federation. In addition to the demand for self-determination, the Bill also sought the transformation of the highly centralised federation into a non-centralised one in which each constituent unit would control the lion's share of its internally-generated revenue (Joseph 1999, p. 366). The Ogoni's agitation for self-determination is about the oil communities having a fair share in the wealth generated by the oil economy.

MOSOP's resistance was perceived by the Nigerian state as constituting a separatist tendency which must be checked, resulting in the killing of Ken-Saro-Wiwa and eight other MOSOP activists by the Sani Abacha junta in November 1993. This brutal murder could not stop the agitation for self-determination, particularly in the Niger Delta.

[2]Osaghae (1995, pp. 330–332) noted that before Independence in 1960, only one Ogoni man held a top political appointment, but since the creation of the River state in 1967, every clan in Ogoni has produced one or more commissioner/minister at the state or federal levels respectively. Osaghae even cited the appointment of the late Ken Saro-Wiwa as Administrator for Bonny during the civil war and later as commissioner for education in the River state, and also in 1993, two of the seven Commissioners in the River State cabinet were Ogoni, and two of the State's three Ministers at the federal level.

The post-1999 period has also experienced the formation of ethnic-based groups aligning themselves with the clamour for self-determination. The Ijaw Youth Council (IYC), for example, vowed to resist such state policies, legislations and practices that prohibit their people from controlling the resources found in their area. This group, particularly inspired by the heroism of the late Isaac Boro, had its demands embodied in the famous 'Kaiama Declaration'.[3] Through this document, the Ijaw people were able to draw the attention of the world to the environmental situation in the region.

The social-economic nexus of the demand for self-determination, which finds expression partly in the unemployment of the people in the region, cannot be ignored. Farmers and fishermen have become unemployed following the destruction of farmlands as well as pollution of available rivers. Most people displaced from their land find it difficult to find jobs in the oil industry due to the capital-intensive nature of the industry. Just like any rentier state, the Nigerian state has minimal control over its oil industry. By virtue of their monopoly on the technology of oil production, the oil giants do resist the acquisition of oil expertise by nationals principally because they want to retain control of operations (Turner 1980, p. 201; Biersteker 1987, p. 241; Ukiwo 2011, p. 285). The reason for this stems from the argument that only the oil giants possess the technical know-how of oil exploration while the local people lack the required skills needed. The issue of environmental degradation could be located within the context of the federal centre's failure to effectively regulate the oil industry. Oil companies operating in Nigeria pay little or no attention to their corporate social responsibilities. Successive governments have failed to make them deliver the expected social and economic benefits to all stakeholders in the oil economy. For obvious reasons, the Nigerian state would not want to jeopardise its relationship with the oil giants. The former is interested in the continuous inflow of oil rents into the Federation Account and the oil companies are equally interested in the unending exploration of the oil, ostensibly, for profit maximisation.

The IYC also decried the relegation of the principle of derivation in the country's revenue allocation system. Additionally, they expressed their disenchantment with the various federal laws, such as the Land Use Decree of 1978 and the various Petroleum Decrees, which deprived the

[3]Kaiama is the hometown of the late Isaac Boro and the IYC meeting that culminated in the release of the 'Kaiama Declaration' took place in Kaiama.

oil-producing states of ownership of land.[4] The IYC position was that these legislations placed them in a disadvantaged position within the Nigerian federation. It is imperative to point out here that the IYC, unlike the Boro-led Niger Delta People's Volunteer Force (NDPVF), wanted the Ijaw ethnic group 'to remain within Nigeria', but also wanted to have control over its resources. In other words, they were demanding a federation that would allow every ethnic group in the country to control the resources found in their area.

The Movement for the Emancipation of the Niger Delta (MEND) is another group that emerged in the Niger Delta region in the post-1999 period. Like the groups before it, MEND's demands were predicated on the country's adherence to a principle of federalism in which every constituent unit will be allowed to have control over the resources found within its jurisdiction. Basically, the group seeks a fiscal system in which a substantial part of the oil-generated revenue will be used to improve the lives of the people in the impoverished region.

It is important to point out that these ethnic-based organisations have succeeded in drawing global attention to the pathetic state of the area. For example, the United Nations Development Programme (UNDP) in one of its reports described the region as 'suffering from administrative neglect, crumbling social infrastructure and services, high unemployment, social deprivation, abject poverty, filth and squalor, and endemic conflict' (UNDP 2006, p. 9). The Niger Delta elite have persistently decried the political and economic marginalisation prevalent in the oil-rich region. Not only that, they constantly accuse their counterparts from the majority ethnic groups who control political power at the federal level of using oil wealth to develop their areas at the expense of the area from where oil is derived (see Naanen 1995; Obi 2006; Osaghae 1995). The point they are making here is that a people whose land produces the wealth that sustains the entire country should not be made to dwell in poverty. Majority ethnic elites are noted for their use of state power to appropriate state resources for themselves and their ethnic groups. By implication, therefore, those who lack access to power also lack access to resources, as the state is the main conduit of appropriation. The people of the Niger Delta constitute a minority in the Nigerian federation, and like other minorities in the country, they are of the

[4]The Land Use Decree of 1978 was aimed at ensuring that the Federal Government has ownership and effective control over land and natural resources across the country.

belief that they lack access to political and economic opportunities. Ben Naanen, a professor of political science and an Ogoni activist, adapted the concept of internal colonialism to describe the relationship between the central Nigerian state and its oil-producing periphery.[5] According to him, the dominant groups in Nigeria and the multinational oil giants transfer resources from the numerically weaker groups (minorities) to develop the dominant areas (majorities), thereby creating an economically advantaged and powerful core, and an impoverished and weak periphery (Naanen 1995, pp. 49–50).

Nigeria's oil-producing minorities have repeatedly argued that Nigeria's fiscal federalism has been unfair to them. Accordingly, they have continued to make a series of demands aimed at liberating themselves from majority hegemony as well as obtaining a fair share of the country's oil-generated wealth. Specifically, they have argued that the systematic downgrading of the derivation principle is a form of internal oppression of the monitories in the federation. More importantly, they believe that they are economically marginalised by the majority ethnic groups.

The North and the Quest for Self-Determination

Northern political leaders had always been in support of the status quo until 1999 when they lost control of the Federal Government to the South, thereby reducing their chances of controlling the national wealth. Increasingly, there were fears amongst the northern elite that the emergence of Olusegun Obasanjo would mark a major disruption in their grip of the national oil wealth—in terms of re-allocation of oil blocs and other business interests. For them, the signs were becoming clear as the government suddenly changed the power structure in the military to the extent that majority of the newly appointed Service Chiefs of the Armed Forces came from the Middle Belt and not from the North. As a strategy

[5]This concept was originally formulated by Michael Hechter in his *Internal Colonialism: The Celtic Fringe in British National Development, 1536–1966* first published in 1975. The work centres on the salience of ethnic identity in which Hechter examines the relationship between England, which he describes as the core and the Celtic fringe, also described as its periphery, in the context of core-periphery relations in the industrial setting. In his conclusion, Hechter predicts that the rise of ethnic solidarity among groups which are disadvantaged by being relegated to inferior positions in a cultural division of labour is inevitable.

to counter the post-military government, the northern elites began to complain of marginalisation in appointments into federal positions and sought self-determination using religion as some states in the north introduced Sharia in 1999.[6] Sharia was not new to the Northerners, especially the Muslims, but its application immediately after the return of the country to democratic rule generated fears of religious domination and discrimination in the states where the system was implemented.

As expected in a deeply divided society such as Nigeria, the re-introduction of Sharia in the core northern states was roundly condemned mostly by non-Muslims in the country, particularly those residing in the affected states, arguing that the adoption of the Islamic law was an abuse of their human rights, and an attempt by these states to adopt Islam as state religion, contravening the provisions of the constitution. They were quick to point to Section 10 of the 1999 Constitution, which states that 'the Government of the Federation or of a state shall not adopt any religion as state religion'. Some even argued that it was a politically motivated attempt by the Northern Muslims to dominate non-Muslims in the country, while others have argued that it was an aberration. For instance, Adamolekun (2005, p. 395) had argued that the move was in contradiction with the established practice in the country, which only allowed customary or Sharia courts to deal with civil matters. On the whole, critics of Sharia had argued that its application was a recipe for religious conflict in the country.

Thus, the move was an assertion of regional autonomy in the religious sphere within a democratic federal Nigeria. Sharia-practising states have not sought to adopt Sharia as a state religion, instead, what they attempted to achieve was self-determination, although not in the mould of secession. It would be foolhardy to think that the northern states would support secession, especially that the country's main natural resource (oil) is in the south. They would not want to jeopardise their source of economic survival, which is national oil revenue. As mentioned in the preceding chapters, Nigeria's federating units depend heavily on the country's centrally-collected oil revenue. This dependence is enough of a constraint on any state, especially the non-oil producing ones.

[6] In October 1999, the Northern State of Zamfara extended Sharia to cover both civil and criminal matters, and eleven other Northern States followed suit. These other states included Bauchi, Borno, Gombe, Jigawa, Kaduna, Kano, Katsina, Kebbi, Niger, Sokoto, and Yobe.

Conclusion

This chapter shows that the deficiency characterising Nigeria's distributive politics drives the conflicts that continuously threaten the survival of the multinational federation. Marginalisation, real or perceived, in the distribution of resources has resulted in the fear factor that has come to characterise the politics. Agitations for secession and self-determination have, more often than not, been championed by ethno-regional groups and federating units who harbour a sense of injustice. These two clichés are used to express disenchantment against the government at the centre, as well as other ethnic groups in the country. As shown in the chapter, the allegation of marginalisation is not limited to the minority groups. However, the agitation for equitable distribution is more intense among the oil-producing minorities whose belief is that they have contributed immensely to the economic survival of the country. It is fair to argue that the clamour for self-determination by the oil-producing states is not just a response to the environmental degradation that characterises the region but also a cry against the scenario of 'want in the midst of plenty'. The clamour for secession and self-determination is a show of dissatisfaction by the aggrieved members of the federal union who desire a fair distribution of Nigeria's oil wealth or put differently, a reform of Nigeria's fiscal federalism.

Clearly, the unhealthy competition for the national wealth, especially the oil-generated revenue is key to the continuous agitation for secession and self-determination. The source of this ruthless competition is, no doubt, the over-centralisation of resources, which is the defining feature of the country.

References

Adamolekun, L. (2005, Summer). The Nigerian Federation at the Crossroads: The Way Forward. *Publius: The Journal of Federalism, 35*(3), 383–405.

Ademoyega, A. (1981). *Why We Stuck: The Story of the First Nigerian Coup.* Ibadan: Evans Brother.

Anber, P. (1967). Modernisation and Political Disintegration: Nigeria and the Ibos. *The Journal of Modern African Studies, 5*(2), 163–179.

Armstrong, R. (1967). *The Issues at Stake: Nigeria 1967.* Ibadan: University of Ibadan Press.

Ayoade, J. (1973). Secession Threat as a Redressive Mechanism in Nigerian Federalism. *Publius: The Journal of Federalism, 3,* 57–75.

Biersteker, T. (1987). *Multinationals, the State, and Control of the Nigerian Economy*. Surrey: Princeton University Press.
Birch, A. (1989). *Nationalism and National Integration*. London: Unwin Hyman.
Buchanan, A. (1991). *Secession: The Morality of Political Divorce from Fort Sumter to Lithuania and Quebec*. Oxford: Westview Press.
Buchanan, A. (1995). Federalism, Secession and the Morality of Inclusion. *Arizona Law Review, 37*(53), 53–63.
Burgess, M. (2006). *Comparative Federalism: Theory and Practice*. London and New York: Routledge.
Collier, P. (2008). *The Bottom Billion: Why the Poorest Countries Are Failing and What Can Be Done About It*. Oxford: Oxford University Press.
Dike, K. (1956). *Trade and Politics in Nigeria, 1830–1885: An Introduction to the Economic and Political History of Nigeria*. London: Oxford University Press.
Dikshit, R. (1975). *The Political Geography of Federalism: An Enquiry into Origins and Stability*. New Delhi: Macmillan.
Gutteridge, W. F. (1969). *The Military in African Politics*. London: Methuen & Co Ltd.
Habtu, A. (2005). Multiethnic Federalism in Ethiopia: A Study of the Secession Clause in the Constitution. *Publius: Journal of Federalism, 35*(2), 313–335.
Hechter, M. (1975). *Internal Colonialism: The Celtic Fringe in British National Development, 1536–1966*. London: Routledge.
Joseph, R. (1999). Autocracy, Violence, and Ethno Military Rule in Nigeria. In R. Joseph (Ed.), *State, Conflict, and Democracy in Africa* . Boulder, CO: Lynne Rienner.
King, K. (1982). *Federalism and Federation*. Baltimore: Johns Hopkins University Press.
Kirk-Greene, A. H. M. (1967). The Peoples of Nigeria: The Cultural Background to the Crisis. *African Affairs, 262*, 3–11.
Kirk-Greene, A. H. M. (1970). *Crisis and Conflict in Nigeria: A Documentary Sourcebook 1966–1970* (Vol. 1). London, New York, and Ibadan: Oxford University Press.
Kirk-Greene, A. H. M. (1975). *The Genesis of the Nigerian Civil War and the Theory of Fear*. Uppsala: Nordic African Institute.
Kymlicka, W. (1995). *Multicultural Citizenship: A Liberal Theory of Minority Rights*. Oxford: Clarendon Press.
Lapidoth, R. (1997). *Autonomy: Flexible Solutions to Ethnic Conflicts*. Washington, DC: United States Institute of Peace Press.
Naanen, B. (1995). Oil-Producing Minorities and the Restructuring of Nigerian Federation: The Case of the Ogoni People. *Journal of Commonwealth and Comparative Politics, 33*(1), 46–78.

Obi, C. (1998). The Impact of Oil on Nigeria's Revenue Allocation System: Problems and Prospects for National Reconstruction. In K. Amuwo, et. al. (Eds.), *Federalism and Political Restructuring in Nigeria*. Ibadan, Nigeria: Spectrum Books Limited and IFRA.

Obi, C. (2006). *Youth and the Generational Dimensions to Struggles for Resource Control in the Niger Delta*. CODESRIA Monograph Series. Dakar: CODESRIA.

Ogoni Bill of Rights. (1990). London and Port Harcourt: Saros International Publishers.

Ojukwu, E. (1969). *The Ahiara Declaration: The Principles of the Biafran Revolution*. Composio, Impresso na Tipografia.

Okonta, I., & Oronto, D. (2001). *Where Vultures Feast: 40 Years of Shell in the Niger Delta*. Benin-City: Environmental Rights Action/Friends of the Earth.

Osaghae, E. (1995). The Ogoni Uprising: Oil Politics, Minority Agitation and the Future of the Nigerian State. *African Affairs, 94*, 325–344.

Osaghae, E. (2003). The State and Ethnic Autonomy in Nigeria. *Regional & Federal Studies, 13*(2), 84–105.

Panter-Brick, S. (1970). From Military Coup to Civil War, January 1966 to May 1967. In S. K. Panter-Brick (Ed.), *Nigerian Politics and Military Rule: Prelude to the Civil War*. London: The Athlone Press.

Turner, T. (1980). Nigeria: Imperialism, Oil Technology and the Comprador State. In P. Nore & T. Turner (Eds.), *Oil and Class Struggle*. London: Zed Press.

Ukiwo, U. (2011). The Nigerian State, Oil and the Niger Delta Crisis. In C. Obi & S. Rustad (Eds.), *Oil and Insurgency in the Niger Delta*. London and New York: Zed Books.

UNGA 61/295. (2008). *United Nations Declaration on the Rights of Indigenous Peoples*.

United Nations Development Programme (UNDP). (2006). *Niger Delta Human Development Report*. Abuja: United Nations Development Programme.

Watts, R. (1966). *New Federations: Experiments in the Commonwealth*. Oxford: Clarendon Press.

Wheare, K. (1963). *Federal Government* (4th ed.). London: Oxford University Press.

Willink, H. (1958). *The Willink's Commission Report* (Nigeria), Reproduced by the League of Human Rights.

CHAPTER 6

Nigeria: A Federation in Search of 'True Federalism'

Introduction

This chapter focuses on the quest of the Nigerian people for a genuine federal system of government or what is referred to as 'true federalism' in Nigerian parlance. Nigeria operates a federal system of government, yet the clamour for 'restructuring' and 'true federalism' continues to dominate political discourse. The chapter aims to bring to the fore the perception of the people with regard to the practice of federalism in the country. In order to achieve this aim, an attempt is made to examine the debates over true federalism and restructuring. The debates represent the search for an authentic federal system. Evidently, the unending over-centralisation of the system, the increasing perception of inequity in revenue allocation and marginalisation of certain sections of the country, lack of fiscal autonomy for the states are some of the factors driving the campaign.

There is no consensus on what 'restructuring' and 'true federalism' mean as ethno-regional groups in the country have their own individual definitions. To some, the twin 'concepts' mean perfecting the existing federal structure while to others; they mean the disintegration of the country. However, according to Osaghae (2018, p. 18), restructuring may be defined as 'a catchall term for the continuous process of adjustments that federal systems undergo in the quest to make them work well and cope with changing demands'. Osaghae argued further that the need

D. Babalola, *The Political Economy of Federalism in Nigeria*, Federalism and Internal Conflicts,
https://doi.org/10.1007/978-3-030-05493-9_6

for restructuring usually arises when existing federal instrumentalities become inadequate to cope with changing political realities. Similarly, true federalism is a new-found term in Nigeria and has been used to mean a more efficient federal system. There seems to be an agreement, especially in the southern part of the country, where the clamour for true federalism is more prevalent, that the practice of federalism in Nigeria does not conform to the fundamental principles of federalism. There is yet the perception that the northern elite wants the status-quo to remain because the present system in which the federal character principle, quota system and majority representation at the federal level, as entrenched in the constitution, favours its interest.

Obviously, the campaign for a reconfiguration of the federal structure predates the Fourth Republic[1] but it became more ferocious immediately after the inauguration of the first civilian administration in the post-military era. In 1999, the governors of the oil-producing states declared that they had resolved to assume full control of the resources found in their jurisdictions 'within the framework of true federalism' (quoted in Elaigwu 2007, p. 285). This declaration is a pointer to the successive federal government's perceived failure to deliver the benefits of the oil economy to the people of the oil-producing states or put differently, a perceived injustice in resource distribution. Although the debates around these issues are championed by ethno-regional elites, they have, nonetheless brought to the front burner of political discourse the efficacy of federalism in the oil-rich federation.

The chapter also discusses how the country's political leaders have, at different times in the history of the country attempted to grapple with the imperfections characterising the federal system, adopting such federal instrumentalities as the federal character principle and state creations. The entrenchment of the federal character principle in the constitution, no doubt, represents a major distributive instrumentality while the constant changing of the geographical structure of the federation is a key

[1] In Nigeria, 'Republic' connotes the period of civilian administration. The Fourth Republic is, therefore, the period of civilian rule that began with the termination of military rule in 1999. The First Republic was the period of the first civilian administration which began from independence in 1960 and came to an end in 1966 when the military sacked the civilian government and installed the first military rule which terminated in 1979. The Second Republic was between 1979 and 1983. The Third Republic was aborted through the annulment of the 1993 presidential election.

structural instrumentality. Despite these measures, the agitations for true federalism continued unabated. The question at this juncture, therefore, is: why have these efforts not yielded the desired results? So, let us begin by examining some of the earlier efforts aimed at ensuring a successful federal system.

State Creation Exercise

At inception in 1954, Nigeria was a federation of three large constituent units: the Northern, Western and Eastern Regions. The Northern Region was bigger in size than the other two combined, and same with the population.[2] It may be argued that the country's three-region federal structure was influenced by its internal natural boundaries but Agbu (2004, p. 32) contends that the arrangement was a deliberate attempt by the British colonial government to bestow the Northern Region with the control of the central government. Either way, the sheer size of the Northern Region was a source of tension in the immediate post-independent period. The North's numerical advantage in the central government gave rise to a situation in which the other two regions perceived themselves as being at a disadvantage in the competition for national resources. This fear was manifested in the disputes over the 1962/1963 national census, where it was alleged that the Hausa-Fulani elite inflated the population of the Northern Region.

Undoubtedly, an arrangement in which one of the constituent units is bigger than others is a sure recipe for disintegration. This point has been made by Osaghae (2018, p. 25) who succinctly noted that the preponderant size of Baganda in the old Ugandan federation and of Jamaica in the defunct West Indian federation contributed to the collapse of these federations. We are not, in any way, suggesting that there is a federation in the world in which the units are equal in size and population but having a federal union in which one unit is bigger than the other two combined is a negation of the principle of federalism. This point had earlier been stressed by Wheare (1963, p. 50), arguing that there is the

[2]According to the 1952/1953 census, the North's population was 16.8 million, East, 7.2 million, West, 6.1 million, and the capital city, Lagos, 267,000 (Post and Vickers 1973, p. 81). Similarly, the 1963 census figures also painted a similar picture as follows: North——29,758,875; East—12,394,462; West—10,265,846, Mid-West—2,535,839; and Lagos-665,246 (Osaghae 1998a, p. 41).

tendency for the powerful unit to overrule the others and even 'bend the will of the federal government to themselves'.

In 1963, the number of constituent units inherited from the British colonial government was increased to four when the Mid-Western Region was carved out from the then Western Region. It may be argued that the Region was created as a response to the agitation of the minorities in the area as the emergent constituent unit composed of the minority ethnic groups of that area. Leaders from the area including the Oba of Benin, Akenzua II and Dennis Osadebay, who later became the first premier of the Region were in the forefront of the clamour for its creation. It is also on record that when the plebiscite was held in the Mid-West, 89% of the registered electors voted for the creation of the new Region (Post and Vickers 1973, p. 89). Some scholars have, however, argued that the creation of the Region was not a genuine effort by the country's political leaders to allay the fear of the minorities but an apparent attempt by the ruling federal coalition of the Northern People's Congress (NPC) and the National Council of Nigerian Citizens (NCNC) to diminish the political strength of its opposition—the Action Group (AG) in the Western region (Ayoade 1988, p. 23; Osaghae 1998a, p. 36; Suberu 1998, p. 281; 2001, pp. 82–85). It was a gang up of the North and the East against the West, they argued. They also buttress their point by making reference to the AG's vehement opposition to the move. Given the zero-sum nature of Nigerian politics, it is fair to concede that the coalition government at the centre took advantage of the regional clamour for the creation of a separate constituent unit. The politics behind its creation notwithstanding, adding the unit to the existing ones did not ameliorate the structural flaw in the federation because the Northern Region retained its numerical strength. As we shall see later, the Mid-West was the only constituent unit to be created by constitutional means as others were created using military fiat.

At the dawn of the civil war in 1967, the Yakubu Gowon regime further divided the country into 12 states.[3] The move was aimed at eradicating the impact of large federating units, as no unit would be big or wealthy enough to overawe the centre. It was also a political strategy to prevent the minorities in the East from identifying with the

[3]The states created included North-Western, North-Eastern, Kano, North-Central, Benue-Plateau, Kwara, Western, Lagos, Mid-Western, Rivers, East-Central and East-Central states.

secessionist Eastern Region. The leadership of the majority ethnic group (Igbo) hoped that the eastern minorities would support the secession. This, however, turned out to be a gross miscalculation as the minorities pitched tent with the Nigerian side hoping that with the defeat of Biafra, and with states of their own, the oil minorities would gain control of the oil resources located in their territory. But the hopes of the minorities were dashed when the federal government reiterated its claim to the ownership of Nigeria's oil, immediately after the war. Nonetheless, the exercise offered the minority groups some prospects for autonomy. As suggested by Bienen (1985, p. 11), the exercise was aimed at getting the support of the minority groups who had always complained of the domination of the major ethnic groups.

Moreover, the creation of additional states diminished the dominance of the Northern Region. It also broke down the hitherto ethno-regional blocs. One striking feature of the states, however, is that they lacked political and fiscal autonomy, negating the federal principle in which component units of a federation are expected to be autonomous within their sphere.

The Murtala Mohammed regime that sacked the Gowon's in 1975 further weakened the federal periphery by creating additional states out of the existing twelve, thereby increasing the number of states in the federation to nineteen.[4] Moreover, as part of the military's agenda to restore democratic rule, the Babangida military regime (1985–1993) created Kastina and Akwa Ibom states in 1987 and another nine in 1991 making the total number of states to be thirty (15 in the North and 15 in the South).[5] Given Babangida's seeming insincerity, especially with regards to the transition process, it may be argued that his regime created those states in an attempt to boost his political support or reduce the opposition to his regime. However, one advantage of the move, as Suberu (1998, p. 284) noted, is that the 30-state structure has the tendency to spare Nigerians a return of the electoral controversy that surrounded the 1979 presidential election over what constituted the two-thirds of the then 19 states of the federation. The re-division

[4]The states were: Anambra; Bauchi; Bendel; Benue; Borno; Cross River; Gongola; Imo; Kaduna; Kano; Kwara; Lagos; Niger; Ogun; Ondo; Oyo; Plateau; Rivers; and Sokoto.

[5]The states were: Abia; Adamawa; Akwa Ibom; Anambra; Bauchi; Benue; Borno; Cross River; Delta; Edo; Enugu; Imo; Jigawa; Kaduna; Kano; Katsina; Kebbi; Kogi; Kwara; Lagos; Niger; Ogun; Ondo; Osun; Oyo; Plateau; Rivers; Sokoto; Taraba; and Yobe.

of the country continued under the Abacha military regime (1993–1998), which transformed the country into its current 36-state structure. Abacha created additional states perhaps to pacify those ethnic groups who were clamouring for states of their own, and possibly to legitimise his regime.

One significant advantage of the division of the country into smaller states is that no state, in its present form, has the political and financial wherewithal to challenge the authority of the federal government to the point of seceding. In addition, the successive state creations partly helped to free the minorities from the domination of the majorities and also provide them with minimal access to the country's distributive system both at the centre and in the states (Osaghae 1991, p. 243). The proliferation of states has given the ethnic minority groups a feeling of having their own autonomous political space. State creations sometimes help to reduce what Hicks (1978) referred to as 'incompatibilities' within states. Incompatibilities create tensions which impact on service delivery in the state. The carving out of Bayelsa state from the then River state is a good example here as the former is made up predominantly of the Ijaw ethnic group.

It may, however, be argued that by allowing some minorities to have their own state, Nigerian leaders have perpetuated the differences that characterised the federal society. Despite having states of their own, which it was hoped would deliver them from majority domination, the minority groups remained marginalised, as the three major ethnic groups still hold sway. This is a vindication of the view held by the Willinks Commission that the solution to the minorities' problems does not lie in state creation. Another disadvantage of state creation is that, contrary to the federal principle that enjoins constituent units of a federation to be financially viable, states so created by successive governments lacked financial viability and hence their absolute dependence on federal transfers. This, in turn, increases the burden of the federal government because the greater the number of less viable states, the more the cost of administering the country as a whole.

The Federal Character Principle

The Federal Character principle seeks to ensure that the composition of federal institutions reflects the federal character, that is, the diversity of the country, and in a similar vein, at state and local government levels, the composition of institutions must be a reflection of the diversity of that state and local government respectively.[6] In other words, the principle aims to promote a 'sense of belonging' among the citizenry, as well as national unity. The principle was first adopted as a state policy and inserted into the 1979 Constitution and reaffirmed in Section 14(3) of the 1999 Constitution. The constitution makers were very much aware that one of the major causes of the civil war was the fear of one ethnic group dominating the federal government. In their thinking, therefore, the fear of domination or exclusion, which has become a feature of Nigerian politics, must be addressed if national unity is to be achieved. This is where the federal character principle becomes useful.

Since the fundamental objective of the principle was to achieve a balanced federation, it assumes equality of states and emphasises equal state representation in the federal government. In practice, every state of the federation is given a share of federal power in one form or another. To this end, the principle represents a catalyst to national unity. According to Mustapha (1986, p. 89), 'no lasting unity can be expected from a situation in which one half of the country... has a large, disproportionate share in the numerous bureaucracies of the country and the social power derivable therefrom'. Similarly, for Adejumobi (2004, p. 218), the principle is 'a consociational formula to engender inclusivity' as well as equal access to the country's resources.

Like many other policies in the multinational federation, the principle is not without its critics. One significant criticism against it is that it shifts the focus of competition from ethnic groups to states as if states reflect ethnic groupings. According to Osaghae (1998b), by taking states rather than ethnic groups as the units to be represented, the principle favoured the ethnic majorities because they have more states than the minorities. The crux of this argument is that the policy favours some ethnic groups against the others and this is antithetical to national unity which the policy was designed to achieve. Sharing this sentiment was Ayoade (1998, p. 115) who argued that the application of the principle has resulted in the fossilisation of ethnic differences. Another argument against the principle is that it negates meritocracy. For example, Oyovbaire (1983, p. 19) criticised the principle for promoting bureaucratic and technocratic

[6]See Section 14(3) and (4) of the 1999 Constitution of Nigeria. For a detailed analysis of the origin and dynamics of the principle, see K. Amuwo et al. (1998, pp. 99–210) and P. Ekeh and E. Osaghae (1989, pp. 111–140).

mediocrity in positions of power. Similarly, a former Attorney General and Minister of Justice of the Federation who was one of the architects of the principle, Chief Richard Akinjide, argued that the policy allows unqualified people to occupy positions of authority.[7] According to him, the policy was entrenched in the Constitution in good faith, but it has been abused.

The Clamour for 'Restructuring' and 'True Federalism'

Although the debates over what constitutes true federalism have taken a geopolitical dimension, they are still relevant to the operation of federalism in the country. So, let us begin with the south-west, a geopolitical zone dominated by the Yoruba ethnic group.

The agitation for true federalism started in the south-west immediately after the annulment of the 1993 presidential elections, believed to have been won by a Yoruba man, the late M. K. O. Abiola. This struggle was initially championed by prominent Yoruba groups localised in the south-west—*Afenifere* and the O'dua People's Congress (OPC).[8] The Yoruba elite had argued that the elections were annulled because their Hausa-Fulani (of the north) counterparts were not willing to concede political power to the south. It was frustrating for the Yoruba elite who were denied federal political power which was within their grasp. With this mindset, they began to call for a sovereign national conference to resolve the issue of political power distribution among the various ethnic groups in the country. This call later changed to a campaign for a 'power shift' to the south. By power shift, they meant an end to the Hausa-Fulani's stranglehold on political and economic power. The OPC went a bit further by clamouring for the creation of the Oduduwa Republic, a campaign aimed at breaking away from the federal union. The OPC's message of secession was less appealing, especially among the Yoruba

[7] Chief Richard Akinjide was a member of the Constitution Drafting Committee (CDC) that drafted the 1979 Constitution. He made this claim in a newspaper interview (*Sunday Tribune*, 18 July 2010).

[8] Oduduwa, sometimes called O'odua, is the ancestor of the Yoruba people. *Afenifere* is a pan Yoruba socio-political organisation formed by the late Obafemi Awolowo in 1951 to protect the interests of the Yoruba ethnic group within the Nigerian state. Likewise, the OPC, which was formed in 1994 as a self-determination movement following the annulment of the 1993 election, has as its objective the safeguarding of Yoruba ethno-nationalist interests vis-à-vis the Nigerian state (Nolte 2007, p. 217).

elite, and by the late 1990s this message completely waned and a shift in emphasis became imminent. As a response to the call for power shift, however, the northern elite collaborated with their counterparts from the south-west to allow for a Yoruba candidate in the presidential elections of 1999.

With a Yoruba man, Olusegun Obasanjo, emerging as the president in 1999, the clamour for power shift became moribund and was replaced with that of 'true federalism'. This is not suggesting that the south-west elite had jettisoned their ill-feeling for their northern counterparts who, in their perception, control the federal centre. By true federalism, the Yoruba elite mean a federal system with a weak centre. That is, a system in which the constituent units are independent of the centre; a federal system that allows for autonomy of the states, especially in the fiscal sphere whereby a substantial part of the proceeds accruable from every state is returned to that state and an agreed percentage contributed to the centre by the states for the responsibility of the federal government; a system in which each state is allowed to manage its affairs as it deems fit; a system that allows the states to have their separate constitution; a system that allows each state to have an independent police if desired; and the right to self-determination, as well as the right to secede.[9]

It is important to point out at this juncture that the idea of having strong federating units with a weak centre together with absolute resource control is not entirely in consonance with federalism. What the elite are rather advocating, without their knowledge is confederacy. A confederation, by definition, is a governmental system where substantial powers remain with the confederal states, and the general government is dependent upon the regional governments (Wheare 1963, p. 32; Watts 1999, p. 8), whereas, in a federation, the central government incorporates regional units into its decision-making procedure on some constitutionally entrenched basis (King 1982, p. 77). Given this clarification, therefore, it may be argued that the elite's idea of federalism shows some misconception of federalism.

For the Igbo ethnic group in the south-east, Nigeria's federal system is characterised by lopsidedness, particularly in the allocation of national

[9]The Yoruba idea of federalism is well articulated in the position paper of Yoruba coalition groups titled, *Regional Autonomy or Nothing*, published in May 2014, and presented at the 2014 national conference organised by the Jonathan-led federal government. Page 5 of the 90-page document summarises their demands.

resources. They have persistently decried the monopoly of the federal centre by the Hausa-Fulani. The point they are making here is that the Igbo are, especially, after the war in 1970, schemed out of the federal power equation. The Igbo criticise what they refer to as non-integration into the mainstream of Nigerian politics since the end of the civil war, citing under-representation in the post-war federal administrations and the armed forces. In addition, the Igbo have also complained of marginalisation in the distribution of federal amenities. This sense of lack of belonging informs the views of some of the ethnic-based secessionist groups like the Movement for the Actualisation of the Sovereign State of Biafra (MASSOB) and the Indigenous People of Biafra (IPOB) that the Igbo people are no longer interested in being part of the union and should be allowed to secede and form the Sovereign State of Biafra.[10] It is important to point out that the campaign for the resurgence of Biafra is not popular among the Igbo elite whose political and business interests cut across the country. This informs the thinking that the Igbo are, perhaps, using secession as a bargaining chip for political accommodation within the multinational federation. Nonetheless, by true federalism, the Igbo elite mean a federal practice that accommodates every ethnic group in the country.

The clamour for restructuring in the Niger Delta region is also borne out of the feeling of deprivation and marginalisation. The elite's demands have been predicated on the argument that the oil economy has been a curse rather than a blessing to the region. The narrative here is that Nigeria's centralised federal system has been responsible for their marginalisation and therefore sought an equitable distribution of centrally oil-generated revenue. Apparently, central to the agitation for a restructured federal Nigeria in this region is the ownership and control of Nigeria's oil wealth. For the Niger Delta elite, true federalism means a federal practice that allows every state in the federation to control the revenue-generating resources found in their territories. Put simply, the agitation here is about restructuring the country's highly centralised federal system. These demands are strikingly similar to those of their south-west and south-east counterparts.

[10] MASSOB was, at inception, a secessionist movement, which aimed to resurrect the defunct state of Biafra but the movement prides itself as a 'non-violent movement with the main goal of achieving self-determination'. For more on the creation, aim and activities of MASSOB, see www.massob.org. IPOB was particularly created as a secessionist movement and it remained so until its proscription in 2017.

It is important to point out that the political demands emanating from the region over time have not been completely ignored. In fact, successive governments at the centre have since the country's independence in 1960, put in place certain measures aimed at solving the problem of underdevelopment that has become a feature of the region. Some of these measures include the establishment of such agencies as the Niger Delta Development Board (NDDB) in 1960, the Niger Delta Basin Development Authority (NDBDA) in 1976, the Oil Minerals Producing Areas Development Commission (OMPADEC) in 1992, the Niger Delta Development Commission (NDDC) in 2000, and the Ministry of Niger Delta Affairs in 2008 (Babalola 2014, pp. 120–123; see also, Omotola 2007). However, these measures proved incapable of dousing the tension created by the disenchantment with what has been perceived as an inequitable federal system. Interestingly, with the emergence of Goodluck Jonathan, an Ijaw man from the Niger Delta, as the President in 2010, the violent agitation for resource control declined but with the emergence of Muhammadu Buhari, a northern Fulani, in 2015, the region began to witness another wave of petro-violence, this time, led by the Niger Delta Avengers (NDA).

As mentioned earlier, the annulment of the 1993 presidential election set the stage for the call for a conference of the ethnic groups in the country to provide solutions to the problems inherent in the federal system. The late military head of state, Sani Abacha responded to this call when he organised the National Constitutional Conference in 1994 but the exercise turned out to be a ruse as the recommendations were not implemented. Similarly, in what appeared to be a response to the incessant campaign for a conference, former President Olusegun Obasanjo also organised the National Political Reform Conference in 2005 but like the one before it, this also turned out to be a wasted effort. In 2014, President Goodluck Jonathan organised another conference christened the National Conference. This was also believed to be a response to the persistent calls for a conference to resolve such knotty issues bordering on the practice of federalism in Nigeria. The Conference was mandated to consider those issues militating against national unity and progress.[11] At the end of the delegates' deliberations, the Conference made some far-reaching recommendations on revenue allocation, resource control,

[11] *Report of the Constitutional Conference* (2014), published by *Premium Times* (Online), p. 44. This is hereinafter referred to as Conference Report (2014).

creation of states, state police, state constitutions, the local government system and many other national issues. Although the conference was a wasted effort as the recommendations were also not implemented but the recommendations are worth examining.

On the vertical revenue allocation, the Conference recommended the following sharing formula: Federal Government—42.5%; State Governments—35%; and Local Governments—22.5% as against the prevailing practice of Federal Government—52.68%; State Governments—26.72%; and Local Governments—20.60% (Conference Report 2014, p. 153). This change represents a reduction in the federal government's share of the Federation Account and an increase in the states' share. A fiscal arrangement like this will definitely diminish the financial strength of the federal government but does not necessarily mean that the states would be powerful enough to overawe the centre. It also has the tendency to enhance service delivery at the sub-national levels. As regards the principles guiding the horizontal revenue allocation, the Conference decided that the percentages given to *population* and *equality of states* in the existing sharing formula be reduced while that assigned to *social development factor* be increased so as to ensure accelerated development of all parts of the country (Conference Report 2014, pp. 153–154).

On the contentious issue of resource control, it would be recalled that the 2005 Conference recommended an increase in the level of derivation to 17% as against the prevailing 13%. The 2014 Conference though recognised the need to review the derivation formula but failed to do so. Instead, it recommended that the Federal Government should set up a technical committee to determine the appropriate percentages for derivation (Conference Report 2014, p. 155). The inability of the delegates to provide a resolution on an issue that is clearly at the heart of the country's fiscal federalism explains the controversy usually attached to the issue. It may, however, be suggested here that an allocation of 13% is grossly inadequate to address the conspicuous underdevelopment characterising the Niger Delta area. Therefore, an upward review would be a good idea. However, an absolute derivation is a rarity in federal countries, perhaps because it has the tendency to put the federal government and the non-oil-producing states at the mercy of the oil-producing states. In Russia, for example, the oil-producing regions get a 5% share of oil revenue while in India, the federal government controls the oil-generated revenue but provides a share to the producing states, and in Malaysia, the central government shares both on-shore and off-shore resources with the producing states (Anderson 2010, p. 46). What this means is that, in these countries, oil, being a gift of nature—a resource no one has actually produced in the economic sense—belongs to the federal government.

The issue of state creation also resurfaced at the Conference. This subject has remained a huge political issue in the country with virtually every ethnic group wanting to have their own separate state. The 1994 Conference recommended the creation of 20 new states while the 2005 Conference recommended none, believing that the 36-state structure was too expensive to maintain. Having examined the reports of the previous conferences, the 2014 Conference recommended the creation of additional 18 states (three per geopolitical zone), and an additional state for the south-east to make the zone have an equal number of states with the other zones, with the exception of the north-west which has seven. The creation of an additional state for the south-east zone was, according to the Report, in the spirit of equity (Conference Report 2014, p. 279). In addition to these, the Conference also recommended that states willing to merge can do so if desired; and that states should be treated as federating units with the right to self-determination, and the right to have their respective constitutions (Conference Report 2014, p. 294).

If approved, Nigeria will become a federation of 54 states. When compared with India, a 25-state federation with a population of about 1.3 billion and the United States with a population of 325 million having 50 states, then 54 states for Nigeria with a population of about 185 million may not be justifiable. Moreover, despite the country's oil-generated wealth, the existing 36-state structure is expensive to run as the states, perhaps with the exception of Lagos, are run with funds from the national revenue. Therefore, creating more states will definitely put additional pressure on national revenue. It should also be noted that creating new states will bring about the emergence of new elites, whose major interest is the appropriation of the state's limited resources (Babalola and Onapajo, in press). Expectedly, creating more states will lead to another round of clamour for more. It should, however, be agreed that creating an additional state in the south-east would ensure parity among the geopolitical zones, which may, in turn, douse the tension associated with the perception of marginalisation among the Igbo ethnic group.

The Conference also recommended the establishment of state police for any state that desires it (Conference Report 2014, p. 257). As noted earlier, some governors are increasingly finding it difficult to maintain law and order in their states partly because they lack the necessary apparatus to do so. Apparently, such governors belong to the group of Nigerians advocating state police. Their argument is that with state police, governors, being the chief security officers of their states would be able to respond to security problems more effectively. There is yet another group which is opposed to the idea on the ground that the states are not economically viable enough to maintain state police. There is also the palpable fear that experience with the present activities of the governors, as regards their treatment of the opposition and outright domination of the political space show that with state police, it is most likely that the country will produce a collection of autocratic state governors (Babalola and Onapajo, in press).

Those who argue that, due to the ruthless nature of Nigerian politics, the country is not ripe for state police may have a point. However, it may also be argued that the benefits outweigh the demerits. It should be remembered that federalism emphasises the territoriality of the federating units as well as the division of power between the federal government and the constituent governments. Therefore, to ensure efficient service delivery at the constituent level, it is not out of order for each unit to have its own governing institutions, and the police service is one of such. In Australia, Canada and India, for example, each state has its own police which are responsible for maintaining law and order at the state and local levels. These countries operate a two-tier policing system in which the national (federal) police exist alongside the state police. Therefore, Nigeria too may operate a two-tier policing system. Policing in Nigeria may be moved from the exclusive to the concurrent list and those states with the financial capability can have their own police. This would epitomise the federal principle of not only self-rule but a genuine shared rule. However, those without adequate resources may rely on the federal police. In Canada, for example, Ontario and Quebec have their own police but provinces without their own separate police are serviced by the national police, the Royal Canadian Mounted Police (RCMP).

On the issue of state constitutions, allowing each state of the federation to have its own constitution to the extent that it does not contradict the federal constitution is in consonance with what is obtained in other federations. It must be noted that federalism emphasises dual sovereignty. Sovereignty is attributed to both the central and the constituent governments. In an ideal federal set up, therefore, each state maintains a degree of sovereignty over its own form of government. In the United States, for example, each state has its own constitution, which describes the structure, powers and operation of the state government. Typically, state constitutions are designed in accordance with the will of the people of that state and often address issues unique to the state. Since a state relates directly to the citizens, drawing authority from them, then the citizens should have the freedom to determine the form of government they desire in their state. Thus, allowing each state to have its own constitution will certainly promote self-rule, which is a source of strength to the state. It is also another core principle of federalism.

As mentioned earlier, the issue of local government system also featured at the conference. It would be recalled that both the 1994 and 2005 conferences recommended that the three tiers of government comprising federal, state and local governments be retained. However, having noted the alleged abuse of the local government system by state governors, the 2014 Conference recommended the scrapping of the current system comprising 774 local governments. Instead, it recommended that states wishing to create local governments may do so and local governments so created should be administered by the state government (Conference Report 2014, p. 281). This recommendation implies that the local government will cease to be the third tier of government and the country will become a two-tier federation. One obvious contradiction in this recommendation is that the same Conference that noted the abuse of the system by state governors now recommended that states can create local governments if considered necessary. This contradiction notwithstanding, local government administration should be a residual matter to be determined only by the state, and the three-tier system should be retained. However, some measures should be put in place to check the excesses of the governors.

While receiving the Report, the President expressed his delight at the successful outcome of the Conference and promised to implement the recommendations (*Daily Trust*, August 22, 2014; *Vanguard*, August 21 2014). Despite the promise, the recommendations were not implemented. It may be suggested that the non-implementation of the recommendations was due to lack of political will. The President was not prepared to jeopardise his political relationship with the northern political leaders, who were, in the eyes of their southern counterparts, not favourably disposed to the conference and its outcome. Another reason may be that he hoped to work on the recommendations when re-elected in 2015. Unfortunately, he failed to secure a second term. There is a group of Nigerians who applaud the outcome of the Conference, believing that the recommendations represent a panacea to Nigeria's problems, especially those related to the operation of federalism. This group continuously pressured the Buhari government to implement the recommendations, which they see as a means to achieving a restructured federation. There is yet another group which finds the recommendations less appealing. It should be remembered that President Buhari and the ruling party (All Progressives Congress, APC) were never committed to the Conference in the first place. In fact, the APC (while in opposition) distanced itself from the Conference, which they believed was a ploy to mobilise support for President Jonathan's re-election bid in 2015. Not only that, the composition of the conference was seen as less democratic as some members were hand-picked by the President and the state governors.

Conclusion

As shown above, the agitations for true federalism apparently indicate that earlier federal instrumentalities aimed at ensuring an efficient federal system are inadequate to remedy the flaws in the system. As mentioned earlier, the federal character principle was designed to ameliorate the problems of marginalisation but it is clear that the application of the principle has generated more questions than answers. While some commentators have praised it for encouraging equity, others have described it as institutionalised favouritism. Irrespective of how it is viewed, however, the principle is an antidote to nepotism. It represents a step towards national unity and integration. Similarly, one would expect the splitting of the country into smaller units to translate into autonomy for the units but the opposite is the case. The proliferation of states has resulted in weak and less viable states, and a powerful centre, accentuating the political and economic centralisation characterising the federal system. With the states losing their fiscal autonomy, the centre becomes the sole distributor of national wealth. Under military rule, in particular, federating units had their autonomy drastically diminished as they take orders from the centre. In addition, the federal government took over certain services hitherto financed by the states. As presently constituted, states in Nigeria are so emasculated that no individual state, perhaps with the exception of Lagos, can survive without federal handouts.

It is clear from the foregoing analyses that every ethno-regional group have their own idea of restructuring and true federalism. Within the context of Nigeria, therefore, restructuring may be defined as the political mechanism through which a desired federal system can be achieved. For example, the Yoruba elite have advocated a return to the old regional system, or what they define as 'regionalism', where the regions were more independent and powerful against the centre. One way to achieve this, they argue, is by having a federation consisting of a central government and regional governments of ethnic nationalities; an arrangement that could be based on the current six geopolitical zones (Regional Autonomy 2014, p. 5). Their argument is that such an arrangement would reduce the excessive attraction towards the centre and any unit not endowed with natural resources would be more creative in their quest for other sources of internally-generated revenue. The Niger Delta elite are advocating a restructuring that will bring about a new revenue sharing formula anchored on full derivation as against the current thirteen per cent provided for in the 1999 Constitution. The Igbo elite are promoting a restructuring that ensures the geopolitical zones have an equal number of states. As presently constituted, every zone comprises of six states with the exception of the north-west which has seven but the south-east has five.

References

Adejumobi, S. (2004). Civil Society and Federalism in Nigeria. *Regional & Federal Studies, 14*(2), 211–231.

Agbu, O. (2004). Re-inventing Federalism in Post-transition Nigeria: Problems and Prospects. *Africa Development, XXIX*(2), 26–52.

Amuwo, et al. (Eds.). (1998). *Federalism and Political Restructuring in Nigeria.* Ibadan: Spectrum.

Anderson, A. (2010). *Fiscal Federalism: A Comparative Introduction.* Oxford: Oxford University Press.

Ayoade, J. (1988, July). *Federalism in Nigeria: The Problem with the Solution.* Faculty Lecture Delivered at the University of Ibadan, Ibadan.

Ayoade, J. (1998). The Federal Character Principle and the Search for National Integration. In K. Amuwo, et al. (Eds.), *Federalism and Political Restructuring in Nigeria.* Ibadan: Spectrum.

Babalola, D. (2014). The Underdevelopment of Nigeria's Niger Delta Region: Who Is to Blame? *Journal of Sustainable Development, 7*(3), 118–228, 120–123.

Babalola, D., & Onapajo, H. (in press). New Clamour for 'Restructuring' in Nigeria: Elite Politics, Contradictions and Good Governance Alternative.

Bienen, H. (1985). *Political Conflict and Economic Change in Nigeria*. London: Frank Cass.

Daily Trust. (2014, August 22). Jonathan Receives Resolutions, Says...Confab Report to Go to N/Assembly, Council of State. https://www.dailytrust.com.ng/daily/top-stories/32470-jonathan-receives-resolutions-says-confab-report-to-go-to-n-assembly-council-of-state. Accessed on January 15, 2017.

Ekeh, P., & Osaghae, E. (Eds.). (1989). *Federal Character and Federalism in Nigeria*. Ibadan: Heinemann.

Elaigwu, J. (2007). *The Politics of Federalism in Nigeria*. London: Adonis & Abbey Publishers.

Hicks, U. (1978). *Federalism: Failure and Success—A Comparative Study*. London and Basingstoke: Macmillan.

King, P. (1982). *Federalism and Federation*. Baltimore: Johns Hopkins University Press.

Mustapha, A. R. (1986). The National Question and Radical Politics in Nigeria. *Review of African Political Economy, 13*(37), 81–97.

Nolte, I. (2007). Ethnic Vigilantes and the State: The O'odua People's Congress in South-Western Nigeria. *International Relations, 21*(2), 217–235.

Omotola, J. (2007). From the OMPADEC to NDDC: An Assessment of State Responses to Environmental Insecurities in the Niger Delta, Nigeria. *Africa Today, 54*(1), 73–89.

Osaghae, E. (1991). Ethnic Minorities and Federalism in Nigeria. *African Affairs, 90*, 237–258.

Osaghae, E. (1998a). *The Crippled Giant: Nigeria Since Independence*. London: Hurst Company.

Osaghae, E. (1998b). Managing Multiple Minority Problems in a Divided Society: The Nigerian Experience. *Journal of Modern African Studies, 36*(1), 1–24.

Osaghae, E. (2018, January). *Restructuring and True Federalism: Nigeria in Perspective*. Convocation Lecture at National Open University (NOUN), Abuja, Nigeria.

Oyovbaire, S. (1983). Structural Change and Political Processes in Nigeria. *African Affairs, 82*(326), 3–28.

Post, K., & Vickers, M. (1973). *Structure and Conflict in Nigeria 1960–1965*. London: Heinemann.

Report of the Constitutional Conference. (2014). Published by *Premium Times* (Online).

Suberu, R. (1998). States' Creation and the Political Economy of Nigerian Federalism. In K. Amuwo, et al. (Eds.), *Federalism and Political Restructuring in Nigeria*. Ibadan: Spectrum.

Suberu, R. (2001). *Federalism and Ethnic Conflict in Nigeria*. Washington, DC: United States Institute of Peace Press.

Vanguard. (2014, August 21). Confab: We have shamed our critics—Jonathan. https://www.vanguardngr.com/2014/08/confab-shamed-critics-jonathan/. Accessed on January 15, 2017.

Watts, R. (1999). *Comparing Federal Systems* (2nd ed.). Montreal and Kingston: McGill-Queen's University Press.

Wheare, K. C. (1963). *Federal Government* (4th ed.). London: Oxford University Press.

Yoruba Assembly, Afenifere Renewal Group and Yoruba Academy. (2014). *Regional Autonomy or Nothing*. https://www.premiumtimesng.com/docs_download/Regional%20Autonomy%20or%20Nothing%20final%20PDF.Pdf. Accessed on April 20, 2015.

CHAPTER 7

Conclusion: Addressing Nigeria's Ailing Federal System

This chapter summarises the discussions in previous chapters and underscores the currency of political economy in analysing the contradictions in Nigeria's federalism. In the 1963 edition of his seminal work, *Federal Government*, the doyen of federalism, Kenneth C. Wheare noted that 'it is too soon yet to judge whether, in practice, Nigeria will provide an example of federal government or not…' (p. 29). In truth, it was too early to judge the performance of a nine-year-old federation. However, as we have shown in this study, the practice of federalism in the multinational federation presently is laden with colossal defects. Nigeria is a federation with a federal constitution, but in practice, the country works as a unitary state. This vindicates Wheare's (1963, p. 20) argument that a country with a federal constitution may operate that constitution in such a way that the government is not federal. Erk (2004, p. 3) similarly observed that the fact that a country is a federation does not necessarily mean that it has the essential attributes of federalism. In other words, there may be a federation without federalism. Nigeria exemplifies this phenomenon.

Having examined the political economy of Nigeria as dominated by oil rents, it is safe to conclude that oil rents and their distribution have contributed largely to the problems inherent in Nigeria's federalism. Earlier researches have demonstrated that resource-rich countries, especially those that are heavily dependent on oil rents, comparatively perform poorly both politically and economically (see Auty and Gelb 2001; Beblawi 1987;

D. Babalola, *The Political Economy of Federalism in Nigeria*, Federalism and Internal Conflicts,
https://doi.org/10.1007/978-3-030-05493-9_7

Brass 2008; Collier 2008; First 1980; Karl 1997; Ross 1999; Mahdavy 1970; White and Taylor 2001). In Nigeria, this problem is further compounded by the country's federal system, which is characterised by a myriad of centrifugal forces, including ethnic diversity and economic disparity among the federating units. It should be noted that the research principally aimed to demonstrate that there is a dialectical relationship between Nigeria's political economy and its federal system, with the former shaping the latter. Painstakingly, this aim has been analysed in the sense that a thorough examination of the interaction between politics and economics in every phase of Nigeria's federal history shows that the political economy of Nigeria shapes its federal system.

This book presents the argument that the inability of Nigeria's federal system to guarantee an equitable distribution of the Federation's resources, particularly, the oil wealth exemplifies the failure of the system, and this failure has resulted from a domestic political economy which entrenches over-dependency on oil, which in turn promotes over-centralisation of political and economic resources, and rapacious leadership. The country's over-dependency on oil has a significant effect on the political economy of the country, which has also given rise to a contentious revenue-sharing practice among the states of the Federation. Nigeria's oil resource abundance has also resulted in the rent-seeking behaviour among the country's elites.

One significant finding in this study is that the over-centralisation of resources is central to the dysfunctional character of Nigeria's federal system. The centralising tendencies that have come to characterise the governmental system, beginning from 1966 when the military first intervened in the country's politics through to the period of the oil boom in the early 1970s, is key to this verdict. Following the civil war and the oil boom, the federal system became centralised as the federal government assumed an overbearing economic role. In its present form, Nigeria operates a 'top-heavy' or 'top-down' federal system as governmental powers and other resources are exclusively concentrated at the centre. The states are not only dependent on the centre; they are subordinate to the centre. This raises the fundamental question about the operation of federalism in Nigeria. The federal government is the arbiter over oil rents, determining which state gets what share and what share should be accrued to the centre. The resultant effect was the emergence of a very strong centre vis-à-vis the units. With the federal centre becoming an arena of competition for access to, and control over oil resources, the 36 states, the 774 local government areas and the Federal Capital Territory (Abuja) become heavily dependent on the federal government. The implication of the regular inflow of revenue from the centre to the sub-national units is that states now find it convenient to ignore efforts at generating any form of internal revenue. This dependence has also limited the states' capacity to resist federal domination. The consequence of the excessive concentration of political and economic powers at the centre is the highly centralised federal system that presently operates.

Over-centralisation of the system has contributed, in no small measure, to the wrangling that has become a permanent feature of resource distribution in the country. Due to the high degree of inequality in size and wealth, a large number of the states lack adequate revenue from independent sources. It, therefore, becomes necessary for them to share from the centrally-collected revenue to enable them to carry out their constitutional duties. This is a guaranteed means to acquire funds to bridge the fiscal gap between independently generated revenue and those required to enable them to perform their duties towards their respective citizens. However, funds from the centre are never enough. This provides a veritable explanation for why the country's revenue allocation system is never free of contention. As pointed out in Chapter 4, the most contentious issue in the history of Nigeria has been the allocation of national revenue to the states.

Another major problem characterising the federal system is the country's over-dependence on oil. The post-colonial economy inherited a legacy of agricultural economy as a major foreign exchange earner. With the oil boom of 1973, however, the economy became transformed into an oil rentier economy as the state became heavily dependent on centrally-generated oil rents. Consequently, Nigeria began to experience low agricultural productivity, a classic syndrome of the Dutch Disease. According to scholars, one significant 'symptom' of this 'disease' is that the availability of foreign exchange through external rents causes the booming sector to draw capital and labour from hitherto productive sectors of the economy such as agriculture and manufacturing (Brass 2008, p. 527; Ross 1999, pp. 305–306; Yates 1996, pp. 27–28). This partly explains why oil wealth has significantly failed to positively transform the living standards for the great majority of Nigerians. As pointed out in Chapter 3, the effects of over-dependence on oil were first felt in the early 1980s when the international price of oil crashed. This resulted in substantial cuts in government expenditure, and a skyrocketing inflation.

Rentierism fuels corruption and this has also contributed in weakening Nigeria's federalism. This assertion reinforces the viewpoint among rentier scholars that economic rents provide some form of magnetic attraction for corruption. The decolonisation process in Nigeria culminated in the transfer of political power to an indigenous pseudo-capitalist class, which was only interested in state patronage rather than any meaningful economic activity. As observed earlier, the First Republic (1960–1966) witnessed a situation in which economic fortunes in the constituent units resulted in increased public expenditures in the units as well as personal aggrandisement of state office holders, who turned state offices into avenues through which they accessed public funds and other forms of patronage. In the immediate post-independence period, politicians took advantage of their access to state office to acquire wealth for themselves. As indicated in Chapter 5, the collapse of the First Republic was not unconnected with the elites' lust for state power and the benefits that come with power. Similarly, the Second Republic (1979–1983) was grossly enmeshed in the politics of patronage. This combined with the oil price crash of the 1980s to plunge the country into a serious economic turbulence. The parlous state of the economy that characterised this period was instrumental to the military termination of electoral politics in 1983. Successive military governments used oil revenues on white elephant projects that were in turn used as conduits for corrupt practices by state officials. Likewise, state office holders at all levels of government in the post-military era have also used their offices to amass wealth for themselves. The post-1999 era lacked the required checks and balances, thereby making corruption the stock-in-trade of politicians. Generally, oil rents provide the avenue for political and economic patronage for those elites who have political power but Nigeria's mass population does not benefit from the abundant oil-generated wealth.

Nigeria's defective federal system is also partly a manifestation of long years of military rule which began in 1966. The emergence of the military on the political stage changed the entire political and economic landscape of the country. As clearly shown, the military sowed the seed of the excessive centralisation that has become a significant feature of Nigerian federalism. The military's handling of the country's fiscal matters particularly deserves adequate attention because even when they left the stage, their legacy continued to haunt the federal system. Fiscal federalism during the period before the military rule was characterised by a fiscally weak central government because the distribution of national revenue among the constituent units was largely based on the principle of derivation, which enhanced regional fiscal autonomy. After the war in 1970, derivation ceased to be the determinant factor in the revenue-sharing formula and the federal government's domineering status was deepened. Moreover, years of military rule did further damage to the country's fragile unity, which the military supposedly sought to defend. The coup and counter-coup that resulted in the 30-month civil war provides an explanation for this. In fact, the wound inflicted upon the country by the war has yet to heal. Given such characteristics as hierarchical authority, command structure, and the suspension of constitutions, military rule is antithetical to federalism. Federalism is predicated upon constitutionalism; it is a constitutional political system, hence, incompatible with military rule. Clearly, military rule left a permanent imprint on the country's federal system, explaining why the military phenomenon cannot be ignored when undertaking an analysis of Nigerian politics in general and that of the federal system in particular.

It is important to reiterate at this juncture that our major finding with regards to the practice of federalism in Nigeria is that the failure of the Nigerian distributive state to ensure an equitable distribution of oil wealth exemplifies the failure of federalism in the country. It could therefore be concluded that the Nigerian federal system's failure to entrench a fair distributive politics forms the crux of the crisis of federalism in the oil-rich federation.

'Prescriptions' for Nigeria's Dysfunctional Federalism

In this book, we have demonstrated that although, federalism in Nigeria has served the purpose of 'holding together' the divergent ethnic groups in Nigeria but it has not brought about a fair distributive politics in the country. The point being made here is that the political framework established to 'cure' the country's ills has become part of the illness. Hence, Nigeria's federal system is in serious need of some political reforms. Therefore, in this section attempt is made to suggest some reforms capable of resolving the flaws. But before doing that, it is necessary to briefly highlight the ones that have been introduced thus far.

Before 1999, when Nigeria returned to civilian rule, the military had embarked upon certain political reforms aimed at remedying the defects in the country's federal system. For example, before relinquishing power in 1979, the military created additional constituent units and also reformed the local government system. The military had hoped that these reforms would diminish the effects of regionalism that brought down the first civilian administration (1960–1966). It was also hoped that the reforms would eliminate the structural imbalance that characterised the pre-military federation. These hopes were however dashed as the inadequacy of these reforms was reflected in the resurgence of ethnic politics during the Second Republic (1979–1983). This structural approach failed to solve the structural problems in the system. Furthermore, the distributive approach, which includes the adoption of various revenue-sharing formulas and the federal character principle, has proved to be inadequate in solving the distributive problems inherent in the system. The federal character principle, though, takes care of the distribution of political resources, such as cabinet positions in government, has not been sufficient to ameliorate ethnic tension in the country. Similarly, no revenue-sharing formula has, in the history of the country's revenue-sharing practice, been acceptable to all the constituent units and ethno-regional groups. It therefore follows that the reforms carried out thus far have been insufficient to remedy the shortcomings of the federal system because the highly centralised system remained unchanged.

Interestingly, Wheare (1963, p. 34) has done the adherents of federalism across the world a favour by advising that, 'while I have maintained that it is necessary to define the federal principle dogmatically, I do not maintain that it is necessary to apply it religiously'. What is implied here is that a federation should be open to adaptation. That is, a federal constitution should be subject to adaptation, amendment and outright replacement where necessary. The point being made here is that political leaders are at liberty to carry out any reform deemed congruent with their own political environment. We need to be reminded that federations are products of negotiations and compromises, and federalism in Nigeria and elsewhere represents a balance between centripetal and centrifugal forces, that is, between the forces of unity and those of disintegration. To fashion out a more functional federal system, therefore, the country's leaders must not shy away from negotiations and compromises. The Australian federation, for example, was formed in 1901 and has endured because the leaders have continued to negotiate and compromise (Hicks 1978, p. 144).

Nigeria's search for 'true federalism' should, therefore, focus on how to achieve a non-centralised federal system. According to Elazar (1987, p. 34), federal polities 'are characteristically non-centralised'. What this implies is that governmental powers are diffused among many centres and not concentrated in a single centre. This is the defining feature of such classic federations as Canada and the United States of America. Therefore, if a non-centralised system is to be achieved in Nigeria, some powers and responsibilities, particularly, taxing powers should be devolved to the states. The distribution of powers should be done in such a way that the federal government concentrates on matters of national interest such as defence, foreign affairs, currency and other similar matters while the state governments focus on such residual functions as healthcare, primary and secondary education. The enormous power controlled by Nigeria's federal centre has continuously created a zero-sum political competition among the regional elites. Moreover, it has made the centre excessively crucial to the lives of the citizens. As presently constituted, the centre is overloaded and that explains why all eyes are on the centre. With decentralisation of economic resources, the states would be in relative control of their resources and be less dependent on the centre.

In order to address the problem of over-centralisation, the country's fiscal federalism should also emphasise revenue generation rather than revenue distribution, as this would ensure the fiscal viability and independence of the states. As in Austria and Germany, revenue sharing in Nigeria also plays a significant role in financing expenditures at all levels of government. The practice is intended to enable the constituent units in particular to possess the capacity to operate maximally. However, states in Nigeria rely heavily on their share of federally-generated revenue as well as grants from the centre. Therefore, any future reform should be tailored towards the states generating own revenue. States not endowed with oil or similar resource should devise strategies to generate revenue from within. Internally-generated revenue should only complement a state's share of federally-collected revenue. Unless this reform happens, the states will continue to operate like an appendage of the federal government.

Another significant aspect of the federal system that needs addressing is the over-dependence on oil which has contributed to the over-centralisation of the system. In order to do this, certain mechanisms must be put in place, and this may include the development of the agricultural sector; the use of oil revenue to generate backward and forward linkages in the economy; saving any excess oil revenue for rainy days; and maintaining disciplined fiscal policies. It is also important for the federal government, which plays a significant role in the distribution of oil rents to devise a mechanism that would safeguard the economy against the volatility of the international oil market. One apparent advantage of reducing the over-dependency is that the centre would cease to be the locus of struggle for economic resources.

Future reforms must, however, ensure the relative supremacy of the federal government. This is in line with the viewpoint expressed by Maddox (1941, p. 1124) that in a true federation, the central authority should possesses a power of decision independent of the wills of the constituent governments. This argument should not be construed to be a suggestion for the perpetuation of the over-centralisation of the system. The point being made, instead, is that a strong centre can coexist with strong states as argued by Watts (1999, p. 8), who defined federation as a state 'combining strong constituent units with a strong general government', each drawing its powers from the people through a constitution. As noted in Chapter 4, contributors to mainstream literature on fiscal federalism are in consensus that the central government should be assigned the most lucrative sources of revenue in the federation. Thus, the practice in Nigeria where the federal government gets the lion's share of the contents of the Federation Account is not an aberration. It should be recalled that the experience of the civil war informed the federal government's decision to continually exercise control over oil resources. Hence, it would be politically and economically suicidal for the centre to give up the control of oil revenue.

It is useful to reiterate that federalism emphasises the need for the federal and the state governments to operate in a coordinate and independent manner. It should, however, be remembered that the federal idea rests on partnership and cooperation among the governments in the federation. This is what 'shared rule' implies. Absolute independence of the state governments (or put differently, a weak federal centre) as being advocated in some sections of the country poses some problems of practical application. The size of the country, as well as its ethnic diversity and economic disparity, requires a relatively strong federal government that would be able to regulate the competition for national resources. Also, the reality of politics in Nigeria requires a federal system that would ensure the relative supremacy of the central government vis-à-vis the state governments. History shows that regional federalism in which the constituent units were economically stronger than the centre also has its attendant consequences, as was demonstrated during the immediate post-independent period.

Future reform must also ensure an equitable distribution of national wealth. The revenue allocation system should be reformed in such a way that an acceptable sharing formula is obtained. Reviewing the vertical revenue allocation formula should also be part of future reform. Reducing the federal government's share of the Federation Account and increasing the states' will change the balance of power between these two tiers of government. It will also help the states in service delivery. The derivation principle must also be given greater recognition, at least on the ground of equity. Already, the narrative, especially in the oil-producing areas, is that the ethnic majority elites have chosen to de-emphasise the principle now that oil has become the country's economic backbone because oil resources are located in the domain of the powerless minorities (Agbu 2004, p. 37; Ejobowah 2000, pp. 40–42; Obi 2006, p. 13). Evidently, jettisoning the principle would exacerbate the conflicts in the Niger Delta, and may produce contagious effects in other geopolitical regions. The present 13% derivation falls short of the expectations of the oil-producing states and an upward review should be considered. However, it should be noted that full derivation has the tendency to change the complexion of the federation in such a manner that the oil-producing states become powerful enough to challenge the authority of the federal government.

The argument that the extra funds aggravate inequality between the oil-producing states and the non-oil-producing ones is not tenable given the contribution of the oil-producing states to the economy of the country. There is little doubt that decades of oil exploration in the region have resulted in a monumental environmental degradation, which impacts on the economic life of the local people who have lost their farmland and waters to either installation of oil infrastructure or to oil spills and in most cases with no adequate compensation. The underdevelopment of the Niger Delta area is clearly a manifestation of Nigeria's paradox of plenty and needs addressing. It is, however, important to emphasise that all the states and the federal centre are entitled to the oil-generated wealth, making absolute derivation not justifiable. As argued by Awa (1976, p. 64), the philosophy of federalism is meaningless if the constituent units are left to fend for themselves such that the rich unit becomes richer and the poor poorer. Moreover, not sharing the oil-generated revenue with the non-oil-producing states could give rise to economic problems in these states, and this may consequently impact on the federation as a whole. In a federation, poverty in one constituent unit may have a contagious effect on another. Therefore, a robust revenue allocation system is vital to the success of the federation and its continued existence.

It is, however, important to stress at this point that the supposed benefits of extra revenue resulting from derivation have been massively eroded by corruption instead of translating into an improved socio-economic well-being for the citizens who have continued to live in poverty in the midst of plenty (Babalola 2014). In other words, the main issue here may not necessarily be about the proportion of oil revenue accruable to the oil-producing states, but how the funds allocated have been utilised. In Nigeria, generally, oil revenue provides the avenue for corruption, which has continued to take its toll on the economy. One significant way to address this issue is to make corruption attract severe penalty. Also, the immunity clause (Section 308) granting state governors and their deputies immunity against prosecution as entrenched in the Constitution should be looked into. Getting the politicians to repeal this section would be difficult but this is one way through which office holders can be made accountable.

Given the multifarious flaws characterising the federal system, one may be tempted to conclude that federalism has failed in Nigeria. And as shown in the preceding chapter, the apparent defects in the system provide the basis for the agitations for a more functional federalism. It is fair to argue at this juncture that the continuous agitations for true federalism are indications that earlier federal instrumentalities aimed at guaranteeing a successful federal system have only yielded minimal results. For example, rather than address the over-centralisation characterising the federal system, the division of the country into smaller units have only reinforced the federal monopoly of oil resources and, by extension, federal fiscal dominance vis-à-vis the states.

Although, when compared with some of the well-established federations such as Canada, Switzerland and the United States, for instance, Nigeria may be described as a dysfunctional federation. It is, however, erroneous to conclude that federalism has failed in the country and should be jettisoned. There is quite a handful of literature on the utility as well as the relationship between 'success' and 'failure' in federal studies (Burgess 2011; Franck 1968; Hicks 1978). Franck (1968, p. 168) has particularly observed the 'semantic hazards' attached to 'federation' and 'failure', while Burgess (2011, p. 191) observed the 'unthinking fashion' in which these two opposite and relative terms have been used in the study of federalism. Let us then begin with the definition of 'failure' as generally used in the literature. According to Franck (1968, p. 170), failure is defined as 'the discontinuation of a constitutional association between certain units of the union, or the end of the negotiations designed to produce such a constitutional arrangement'. For Franck, therefore, the disintegration of such federations as Rhodesia and Nyasaland (1953–1963) and the West Indies (1958–1962), as well as the East African federalising project which died at conception represent failure.[1] What may be deduced here is that these federations 'failed' because they died prematurely and could not achieve the goals their founders had set for them. Following on from Franck, and as advised by Burgess (2011, pp. 189–206), success and failure should be measured 'in relation to the declared goals and purposes of each federal state'. So what purpose was the Nigerian federation created to serve?

The primary goal of the Nigerian federation was ostensibly to hold together the disparate ethnic groups within the country. Failure to achieve this daunting goal, therefore, will amount to a failure of federalism in the country. Federalism was adopted in Nigeria because of the capacity of the system to accommodate the country's array of diversities. Given this goal, therefore, one may argue that, on the one hand, the continued existence of the country is a success, despite its inherent centrifugal forces such as a high degree of ethnic and religious diversity, and the abundance of oil resources which could easily be a catalyst for disintegration. On the other hand, the inability of the federal system to ensure an equitable distribution of resources is a failure. Therefore, 'failure' in relation to the Nigerian federation is defined as the inability of the federal political system to guarantee an equitable distributive politics, while 'success' is defined as the continued existence of the federation.

Despite its shortcomings, Nigeria's experience shows that federalism is better equipped to accommodate sub-nationalism, explaining why past leaders (with the exception of the first military leader, General Aguiyi Ironsi) favoured the federal idea. The present crop of leaders has, as well, continuously made the explicit case for federalism. As shown in Chapter 2, the multifaceted differences that exist among the peoples of Nigeria made the choice of federalism almost inevitable. Besides, history also shows that a unitary system of government is not feasible. The brief

[1] For an insightful discussion on why these federations failed, see Franck (1968, pp. 167–199).

experiment with a unitary system following the military coup in January 1966 proved disastrous, leading to the counter-coup of July 1966 and subsequently, the civil war in 1967. Obviously, the solution to Nigeria's problems lies with federalism.

We have been able to demonstrate in this study that Nigerian federalism is defective and the Federation may be described as dysfunctional. This is not suggesting that the Federation has reached a dead-end; there is still light at the end of the tunnel if certain reforms, including those suggested thus far, are carried out. No federation is stress-free. For example, the seemingly unending conflict between the French-speaking peoples mainly located in Quebec and the dominant English-speaking peoples scattered around the country represents a dent in the operation of federalism in Canada. What Nigeria's federal system needs is an audacious political reform. Reforming the federal system will help to address those knotty issues bordering on the practice of federalism, especially those not fully resolved at the time of the federal formation.

The Nigerian federation has endured despite its in-built complexities and federalism has become the basis for the country's stability. The problem with the Nigerian state is not federalism but the failure to operate it properly. Therefore, as the political leaders have done throughout the post-independence history of the country, they should work out ways to improve upon the current federal system. Ethno-regional demands for a more functional federal system will not go away until the elites reform the institutions and structures of the state to produce a genuine federation.

This book has contributed to our understanding of federalism in Nigeria, and its main theoretical contribution lies in the use of the rentier political economy approach. This approach has significantly aided our understanding of the relative failure of federalism in Nigeria. It has also helped to demonstrate that there is a dialectical relationship between Nigeria's political economy and its federal system, with the former shaping the latter. Thus, we have been able to bring to the fore the main political and economic aspects of Nigerian federalism, and their interactions with Nigeria's federal society. Having looked beyond the traditional approaches to federalism we have provided a new entry point to the study of federalism in Nigeria. Hopefully, this will have an impact on students of federalism, that to understand fully the workings of any federal system, one needs to recognise that federalism transcends the purview of political institutions, the legal relations between the centre and the federating units, the distribution of political power, or the accommodation of the diverse groups in the federation; it is also about the political economy of the federation. It may therefore be appropriate to claim here that our findings have justified the use of the political economy approach, particularly the rentier theory, because using either the institutional/constitutional, sociological or political approach alone would have been inadequate to explain the failure of federalism in Nigeria.

It is imperative to point out here that although, this study has significantly contributed to our understanding of the political economy of federalism in Nigeria, but there lays an array of unexplored research territory. An important area for further research would be to engage in a comparative analysis of the interaction between politics and economics in Nigeria and that of an established multinational federation such as Canada. A study of the political economy of federalism in Canada may be theoretically and empirically illuminating to the theory and practice of federalism in Nigeria.

References

Agbu, O. (2004). Re-inventing Federalism in Post-transition Nigeria: Problems and Prospects. *Africa Development, XXIX*(2), 26–52.

Auty, R., & Gelb, A. (2001). Political Economy of Resource-Abundant States. In R. M. Auty (Ed.), *Resource Abundance and Economic Development.* Oxford: Oxford University Press.

Awa, E. (1976). *Issues in Federalism.* Benin City: Ethiope Publishing Corporation.

Babalola, D. (2014). The Underdevelopment of Nigeria's Niger Delta Region: Who Is to Blame? *Journal of Sustainable Development, 7*(3), 118–228, 120–123.

Beblawi, H. (1987). The Rentier State in the Arab World. In H. Beblawi & G. Luciani (Eds.), *The Rentier State.* London: Croom Helm.

Brass, J. N. (2008). Djibouti's Unusual Resource Curse. *Journal of Modern African Studies, 46*(4), 523–545.

Burgess, M. (2011). Success and Failure in Federation: Comparative Perspectives. In T. J. Courchene, et al. (Eds.), *The Federal Idea: Essays in Honour of Ronald L. Watts.* Montreal: Mcgill-Queen's University Press.

Collier, P. (2008). *The Bottom Billion: Why the Poorest Countries Are Failing and What Can Be Done About It.* Oxford: Oxford University Press.

Ejobowah, J. (2000). Who Owns the Oil? The Politics of Ethnicity in the Niger Delta of Nigeria. *Africa Today, 47*(1) (Winter), 29–47, 40–42.

Elazar, D. (1987). *Exploring Federalism*. Tuscaloosa: The University of Alabama Press.
Erk, J. (2004). Austria: A Federation Without Federalism. *Publius: The Journal of Federalism, 34*(1), 1–20.
First, R. (1980). Libya: Class and State in an Oil Economy. In P. Nore & T. Turner (Eds.), *Oil and Class Struggle*. London: Zed Press.
Franck, T. (1968). *Why Federations Fail: An Inquiry into the Requisites for Successful Federalism*. New York: New York University Press.
Hicks, U. (1978). *Federalism: Failure and Success—A Comparative Study*. London and Basingstoke: Macmillan.
Karl, T. (1997). *The Paradox of Plenty: Oil Booms and Petro-States*. Berkeley: University of California Press.
Maddox, W. (1941, December). The Political Basis of Federation. *The American Political Science Review, 35* (6), 1120–1127.
Mahdavy, H. (1970). The Patterns and Problems of Economic Development in Rentier States: The Case of Iran. In M. A. Cook (Ed.), *Studies in the Economic History of the Middle East*. London: Oxford University Press.
Obi, C. (2006). *Youth and the Generational Dimensions to Struggles for Resource Control in the Niger Delta*. CODESRIA Monograph Series. Dakar: CODESRIA.
Ross, M. (1999, January). The Political Economy of the Resource Curse. *World Politics, 51*, 279–322.
Watts, R. (1999). *Comparing Federal Systems* (2nd ed.). Montreal and Kingston: McGill-Queen's University Press.
Wheare, K. (1963). *Federal Government* (4th ed.). London: Oxford University Press.
White, G., & Taylor, S. (2001). Well-Oiled Regimes: Oil & Uncertain Transitions in Algeria & Nigeria. *Review of African Political Economy, 28*(89), 323–344.
Yates, D. (1996). *The Rentier State in Africa: Oil Rent Dependency and Neocolonialism in the Republic of Gabon*. Trenton: Africa World Press.

Bibliography

Abah, B. (2006, March/April). Nigeria Faces Conflict: Can Sharia Law Work in a Multi-religious Federation? *Federations: A Publication of the Forums of Federations, 5*(2), 3–4.

Aboyade, O. (1966). *Foundations of an African Economy: A Study of Investment and Growth in Nigeria*. New York, Washington, and London: Praeger.

Adamolekun, L. (2005). The Nigerian Federation at the Crossroads: The Way Forward. *Publius: The Journal of Federalism, 35*(3) (Summer), 383–405.

Adedeji, A. (1969). *Nigerian Federal Finance: Its Development, Problems and Prospects*. London: Hutchinson Educational.

Adejumobi, S. (2004). Civil Society and Federalism in Nigeria. *Regional & Federal Studies, 14*(2), 211–231.

Ademoyega, A. (1981). *Why We Stuck: The Story of the First Nigerian Coup*. Ibadan: Evans Brother.

Afigbo, A. (1991). Background to Nigerian Federalism: Federal Features in the Colonial State. *Publius: The Journal of Federalism, 21*(4), 13–29.

Agbu, O. (2004). Re-inventing Federalism in Post-transition Nigeria: Problems and Prospects. *Africa Development, XXIX*(2), 26–52.

Aina, A. (1986). What Is Political Economy? In *The Nigerian Economy: A Political Economy Approach*. Essex: Longman Group.

Aiyede, R. (2009, June). The Political Economy of Fiscal Federalism and the Dilemma of Constructing a Developmental State in Nigeria. *International Political Science Review, 30*(3), 249–269.

D. Babalola, *The Political Economy of Federalism in Nigeria*, Federalism and Internal Conflicts, https://doi.org/10.1007/978-3-030-05493-9

Ake, C. (1981). *A Political Economy of Africa*. Harlow: Longman.

Amin, S. (1981). Underdevelopment and Dependence in Black Africa: Origins and Contemporary Forms. In D. Cohen & J. Daniel (Eds.), *Political Economy of Africa: Selected Readings*. Harlow and Essex: Longman Group.

Amuwo, et al. (Eds.). (1998). *Federalism and Political Restructuring in Nigeria*. Ibadan: Spectrum.

Anber, P. (1967). Modernisation and Political Disintegration: Nigeria and the Ibos. *The Journal of Modern African Studies, 5*(2), 163–179.

Anderson, A. (2010). *Fiscal Federalism: A Comparative Introduction*. Oxford: Oxford University Press.

Armstrong, R. (1967). *The Issues at Stake: Nigeria 1967*. Ibadan: University of Ibadan Press.

Ashwe, C. (1986). *Fiscal Federalism in Nigeria* (Research Monograph No. 46). Canberra: Centre for Research on Federal Financial Relations, Australian National University.

Auty, R., & Gelb, A. (2001). Political Economy of Resource-Abundant States. In R. M. Auty (Ed.), *Resource Abundance and Economic Development*. Oxford: Oxford University Press.

Awa, E. (1964). *Federal Government in Nigeria*. Berkeley and Los Angeles: University of California Press.

Awa, E. (1976). *Issues in Federalism*. Benin City: Ethiope Publishing Corporation.

Awolowo, O. (1947). *Path to Nigerian Freedom*. London: Faber and Faber.

Ayoade, J. (1973). Secession Threat as a Redressive Mechanism in Nigerian Federalism. *Publius: The Journal of Federalism, 3*, 57–75.

Ayoade, J. (1988, July). *Federalism in Nigeria: The Problem with the Solution*. Faculty Lecture Delivered at the University of Ibadan, Ibadan.

Ayoade, J. (1998). The Federal Character Principle and the Search for National Integration. In K. Amuwo, et al. (Eds.), *Federalism and Political Restructuring in Nigeria*. Ibadan: Spectrum.

Babalola, D. (2014). The Underdevelopment of Nigeria's Niger Delta Region: Who Is to Blame? *Journal of Sustainable Development, 7*(3), 118–228, 120–123.

Babalola, D. (2018). Ethnicity, Ethnic Conflict and the Elusive Quest for Peace in Post-military Nigeria. In D. Babalola & H. Onapajo (Eds.), *Nigeria, a Country Under Siege: Issues of Conflict and Its Management*. Newcastle upon Tyne: Cambridge Scholars Publishing.

Babalola, D., & Onapajo, H. (in press). New Clamour for 'Restructuring' in Nigeria: Elite Politics, Contradictions and Good Governance Alternative.

Baker, P. (1984). *The Economics of Nigerian Federalism*. Washington, DC: Battelle Memorial Institute.

Balewa, T. (1964). *Mr Prime Minister*. Lagos: Government Printer.

Ballard, J. (1971, October). Administrative Origins of Nigerian Federalism. *African Affairs, 70*(281), 333–348.

Bangura, Y., Mustapha, A. R., & Adamu, S. (1986). The Deepening Economic Crisis and Its Political Implications. In S. Mohammed & T. Edoh (Eds.), *Nigeria: A Republic in Ruins*. Zaria: Gaskiya Corporation.

Beblawi, H. (1987). The Rentier State in the Arab World. In H. Beblawi & G. Luciani (Eds.), *The Rentier State*. London: Croom Helm.

Beblawi, H., & Luciani, G. (1987). Introduction. In H. Beblawi & G. Luciani (Eds.), *The Rentier State*. London: Croom Helm.

Bello, A. (1962). *My Life: An Autobiography*. Cambridge: University Press.

Bienen, H. (1985). *Political Conflict and Economic Change in Nigeria*. London: Frank Cass.

Biersteker, T. (1987). *Multinationals, the State, and Control of the Nigerian Economy*. Surrey: Princeton University Press.

Birch, A. (1966). Approaches to the Study of Federalism. *Political Studies, 14*, 15–33.

Birch, A. (1989). *Nationalism and National Integration*. London: Unwin Hyman.

Boadway, R., & Shah, A. (2009). *Fiscal Federalism: Principles and Practice of Multiorder Governance*. Cambridge: Cambridge University Press.

Brass, J. N. (2008). Djibouti's Unusual Resource Curse. *Journal of Modern African Studies, 46*(4), 523–545.

Buchanan, A. (1991). *Secession: The Morality of Political Divorce from Fort Sumter to Lithuania and Quebec*. Oxford: Westview Press.

Buchanan, A. (1995). Federalism, Secession and the Morality of Inclusion. *Arizona Law Review, 37*(53), 53–63.

Burgess, M. (1993). Federalism and Federation: A Reappraisal. In M. Burgess & A.-G. Gagnon (Eds.), *Comparative Federalism and Federation: Competing Traditions and Future Directions*. New York and London: Harvester Wheatcheaf.

Burgess, M. (1999). Obstinate or Obsolete? The State of the Canadian Federation. *Regional & Federal Studies, 9*(2), 1–15.

Burgess, M. (2006). *Comparative Federalism: Theory and Practice*. London and New York: Routledge.

Burgess, M. (2007). The British Tradition of Federalism: Nature, Meaning and Significance. In S. Henig (Ed.), *Federalism and the British*. London: Federal Trust.

Burgess, M. (2011). Success and Failure in Federation: Comparative Perspectives. In T. J. Courchene, et al. (Eds.), *The Federal Idea: Essays in Honour of Ronald L. Watts*. Montreal: McGill-Queen's University Press.

Burgess, M. (2012a). *Federalism in Africa: An Essay on the Impacts of Cultural Diversity, Development and Democracy*. The Federal Idea: A Quebec Think Tank on Federalism.

Burgess, M. (2012b). *In Search of the Federal Spirit: New Theoretical and Empirical Perspectives in Comparative Federalism*. Oxford: Oxford University Press.

Coleman, J. (1958). *Nigeria: Background to Nationalism*. Los Angeles: University of California Press.

Collier, P., & Hoeffler, A. (1998). On Economic Causes of Civil War. *Oxford Economic Articles, 50*(4), 563–573.

Collier, P. (2008). *The Bottom Billion: Why the Poorest Countries Are Failing and What Can Be Done About It*. Oxford: Oxford University Press.

Collin, P., Turner, T., & Williams, G. (1976). Capitalism and the Coup. In G. Williams (Ed.), *Nigeria: Economy and Society*. London: Rex Collings.

Daily Trust. (2014, August 22). Jonathan Receives Resolutions, Says…Confab Report to Go to N/Assembly, Council of State. https://www.dailytrust.com.ng/daily/top-stories/32470-jonathan-receives-resolutions-says-confab-report-to-go-to-n-assembly-council-of-state. Accessed on January 15, 2017.

Danjuma, T. Y. (1996). Revenue Sharing and the Political Economy of Nigerian Federalism. In Elaigwu & Akindele (Eds.), *Federalism and Nation Building in Nigeria: The Challenges of the 21st Century*. Abuja: Nigerian Journal of Inter-Governmental Relations.

Davis, R. (1978). *The Federal Principle: A Journey Through Time in Quest of Meaning*. Berkeley, Los Angeles, and London: University of California Press.

Dent, M. (2000). Nigeria: Federalism and Ethnic Rivalry. *Parliamentary Affairs, 53*, 157–168.

Diamond, L. (1988). *Class, Ethnicity and Democracy in Nigeria: The Failure of the First Republic*. London: Macmillan.

Diamond, L. (1991). Nigeria's Search for a New Political Order. *Journal of Democracy, 2*(2), 54–69.

Dike, K. (1956). *Trade and Politics in Nigeria, 1830–1885: An Introduction to the Economic and Political History of Nigeria*. London: Oxford University Press.

Dikshit, R. (1975). *The Political Geography of Federalism: An Enquiry into Origins and Stability*. New Delhi: Macmillan.

Duchacek, I. (1970). *Comparative Federalism: The Territorial Dimension of Politics, Lanham*. London: University Press of America.

Eatwell, J., Milgate, M., & Newman, P. (Eds.). (1987). *The New Palgrave Dictionary of Economics*. London and Basingstoke: Macmillan.

Ejobowah, J. (2000, Winter). Who Owns the Oil? The Politics of Ethnicity in the Niger Delta of Nigeria. *Africa Today, 47*(1), 29–47.

Ejobowah, J. (2010). Territorial Pluralism: Assessing the Ethnofederal Variant in Nigeria. *Regional and Federal Studies, 20*(2), 251–274.

Ekeh, P., & Osaghae, E. (Eds.). (1989). *Federal Character and Federalism in Nigeria*. Ibadan: Heinemann.

Ekpo, A. (2006). Federal Republic of Nigeria. In A. Shah (Ed.), *The Practice of Fiscal Federalism: Comparative Perspectives* (A Global Dialogue on Federalism, Vol. 4). Montreal: McGill-Queen's University Press.

Elaigwu, J. (2002). Federalism in Nigeria's New Democratic Polity. *Publius: The Journal of Federalism, 32*(2), 79–83.

Elaigwu, J. (2007). *The Politics of Federalism in Nigeria*. London: Adonis & Abbey Publishers.

Elazar, D. (1973, Autumn). First Principles. *Publius: The Journal of Federalism, 3*(2), 1–10.

Elazar, D. (1987). *Exploring Federalism*. Alabama: The University of Alabama Press.

Eleazu, U. (1977). *Federalism and Nation Building: The Nigerian Experience 1954–1964*. Devon: Arthur H. Stockwell.

Erk, J. (2004). Austria: A Federation Without Federalism. *Publius, The Journal of Federalism, 34*(1), 1–20.

FGN. (1999). *Constitution of the Federal Republic of Nigeria*. Lagos: Federal Government Press.

First, R. (1980). Libya: Class and State in an Oil Economy. In P. Nore & T. Turner (Eds.), *Oil and Class Struggle*. London: Zed Press.

Franck, T. (1968). *Why Federations Fail: An Inquiry into the Requisites for Successful Federalism*. New York: New York University Press.

Freinkman, L. (2008). Intergovernmental Relations in Nigeria: Improving Service Delivery in Core Sectors. In J. Elaigwu (Ed.), *Fiscal Federalism in Nigeria: Facing the Challenges of the Future*. London: Adonis & Abbey Publishers.

Friedrich, C. (1968). *Trends of Federalism in Theory and Practice*. New York: Praeger.

Galadima, H. (2008). Division of Powers and Responsibilities (Including Tax Powers) in Nigeria. In J. Elaigwu (Ed.), *Fiscal Federalism in Nigeria: Facing the Challenges of the Future*. London: Adonis & Abbey Publishers.

Galligan, B. (1995). *A Federal Republic: Australia's Constitutional System of Government*. Cambridge: Cambridge University Press.

Graf, W. (1988). *The Nigerian State: Political Economy, State, Class and Political System in the Post-Colonial Era*. London: Currey.

Habtu, A. (2005). Multiethnic Federalism in Ethiopia: A Study of the Secession Clause in the Constitution. *Publius: Journal of Federalism, 35*(2), 313–335.

Hechter, M. (1975). *Internal Colonialism: The Celtic Fringe in British National Development, 1536–1966*. London: Routledge.

Hicks, U. (1978). *Federalism: Failure and Success—A Comparative Study*. London and Basingstoke: Macmillan.

Horowitz, D. (2000). *Ethnic Groups in Conflict*. London: University of California Press.

Ibrahim, J. (1991). Religion and Political Turbulence in Nigeria. *Journal of Modern African Studies, 29*(1), 115–136.

International Crisis Group (ICG). (2006, July 19). *Nigeria: Want in the Midst of Plenty* (Crisis Group Africa Report, No. 113).

Iyoha, M. (2008). Fiscal Federalism: Towards Coping with and Resolving Future Challenges. In J. Elaigwu (Ed.), *Fiscal Federalism in Nigeria: Facing the Challenges of the Future*. London: Adonis & Abbey Publishers.

Jinadu, A. (2016). The Federal Idea in Nigeria: From the Beginnings to 1946. In O. Ibeanu & M. J. Kuna (Eds.), *Nigerian Federalism: Continuing Quest for Stability and Nation-Building*. Ibadan: Safari Books.

Joseph, R. (1999). Autocracy, Violence, and Ethno Military Rule in Nigeria. In R. Joseph (Ed.), *State, Conflict, and Democracy in Africa*. Boulder, CO: Lynne Rienner.

Karl, T. (1997). *The Paradox of Plenty: Oil Booms and Petro-States*. Berkeley: University of California Press.

Keil, S. (2013). *Multinational Federalism in Bosnia and Herzegovina*. Surrey: Ashgate.

Keller, E. (2002). Ethnic Federalism, Fiscal Reform, Development and Democracy in Ethiopia. *African Journal of Political Science, 7*(1), 21–50.

Kenny, J. (1996). Sharia and Christianity in Nigeria: Islam and a 'Secular' State. *Journal of Religion in Africa, 26*(4), 338–364.

Khan, S. (1994). *Nigeria: the Political Economy of Oil*. Oxford: Oxford University Press.

King, K. (1982). *Federalism and Federation*. Baltimore: Johns Hopkins University Press.

Kirk-Greene, A. H. M. (1967). The Peoples of Nigeria: The Cultural Background to the Crisis. *African Affairs, 262*, 3–11.

Kirk-Greene, A. H. M. (1970). *Crisis and Conflict in Nigeria: A Documentary Sourcebook 1966–1970* (Vol. 1). London, New York, and Ibadan: Oxford University Press.

Kirk-Greene, A. H. M. (1975). *The Genesis of the Nigerian Civil War and the Theory of Fear*. Uppsala: Nordic African Institute.

Kirk-Greene, A. H. M., & Rimmer, D. (1981). *Nigeria since 1970: A Political and Economic Outline*. London: Hodder & Stoughton.

Kymlicka, W. (1995). *Multicultural Citizenship: A Liberal Theory of Minority Rights*. Oxford: Clarendon Press.

Lapidoth, R. (1997). *Autonomy: Flexible Solutions to Ethnic Conflicts*. Washington, DC: United States Institute of Peace Press.

Livingston, W. (1952). A Note on the Nature of Federalism. *Political Science Quarterly, 67*, 81–95.

Livingston, W. (1956). *Federalism and Constitutional Change*. Oxford: Clarendon Press.

Luciani, G. (1987). Allocation vs. Production States. In H. Beblawi & G. Luciani (Eds.), *The Rentier State*. London: Croom Helm.

Luciani, G. (Ed.). (1990). *The Arab State*. Berkeley and Los Angeles: University of California Press.

Macmahon, A. (1962). The Problems of Federalism: A Survey. In A. Macmahon (Ed.), *Federalism: Mature and Emergent*. New York: Russell & Russell.

Macmahon, A. (1972). *Administering Federalism in a Democracy*. New York: Oxford University Press.

Maddox, W. (1941, December). The Political Basis of Federation. *The American Political Science Review, 35*(6), 1120–1127.

Mahdavy, H. (1970). The Patterns and Problems of Economic Development in Rentier States: the Case of Iran. In M. A. Cook (Ed.), *Studies in The Economic History of The Middle East*. London: Oxford University Press.

May, J. (1969). *Federalism and Fiscal Adjustment*. Oxford: Clarendon press.

McKay, D. (2004). William Riker on Federalism: Sometimes Wrong But More Right Than Anyone Else? *Regional & Federal Studies, 14*(2), 167–186.

Mustapha, A. R. (1986). The National Question and Radical Politics in Nigeria. *Review of African Political Economy, 13*(37), 81–97.

Naanen, B. (1995). Oil-Producing Minorities and the Restructuring of Nigerian Federation: The Case of the Ogoni People. *Journal of Commonwealth and Comparative Politics, 33*(1), 46–78.

Nigeria. (1953). *Report of the Fiscal Commissioner on the Financial Effects of the Proposed New Constitutional Arrangements, Cmd.9026*. Report by Louis Chick. Lagos: Government Printers.

Nigeria. (1958). *Preliminary Report of the Fiscal Commission*. Report by J. Raisman & Trees. Lagos: Government Printers.

Nigeria. (1965). *Fiscal Review Commission*. Report by K. J. Binns. Lagos: Government Printers.

Nnoli, O. (1995). *Ethnicity and Development in Nigeria*. Aldershot: Avebury.

Nolte, I. (2002, Spring). Federalism and Communal Conflict in Nigeria. *Regional and Federal Studies, 12*(1), 171–192.

Nolte, I. (2007). Ethnic Vigilantes and the State: The O'odua People's Congress in South-Western Nigeria. *International Relations, 21*(2), 217–235.

Nwabueze, B. (2007). *How President Obasanjo Subverted Nigeria's Federal System*. Ibadan, Abuja, and Owerri: Gold Press Limited.

Oates, W. (1972). *Fiscal Federalism*. New York: Harcourt Brace Jovanorich.

Oates, W. (1999). An Essay on Fiscal Federalism. *Journal of Economic Literature, XXXVII*(9), 1120–1149.

Obi, C. (1998). The Impact of Oil on Nigeria's Revenue Allocation System: Problems and Prospects for National Reconstruction. In K. Amuwo, et al. (Eds.), *Federalism and Political Restructuring in Nigeria*. Ibadan, Nigeria: Spectrum Books Limited and IFRA.

Obi, C. (2006). *Youth and the Generational Dimensions to Struggles for Resource Control in the Niger Delta*. CODESRIA Monograph Series. Dakar: CODESRIA.

Ogoni Bill of Rights. (1990). London and Port Harcourt: Saros International Publishers.

Ojukwu, E. (1969). *The Ahiara Declaration: The Principles of the Biafran Revolution*. Composio, Impresso na Tipografia.

Okonta, I., & Oronto, D. (2001). *Where Vultures Feast: 40 Years of Shell in the Niger Delta*. Benin City: Environmental Rights Action/Friends of the Earth.

Olaloku, A. F. (1979). Nigerian Federal Finance: Issues and Choices. In B. Akinyemi, et al. (Eds.), *Readings on Federalism*. Lagos, Nigeria: The Nigerian Institute of International Affairs (NIIA).

Omotola, J. (2007). From the OMPADEC to NDDC: An Assessment of State Responses to Environmental Insecurities in the Niger Delta, Nigeria. *Africa Today, 54*(1), 73–89.

Onapajo, H. (2012). Politics for God: Religion, Politics and Conflict in Democratic Nigeria. *The Journal of Pan African Studies, 4*(9), 42–66.

Osadolor, O. (1998). The Development of the Federal Idea and the Federal Framework, 1914–1960. In K. Amuwo, et al. (Eds.), *Federalism and Political Restructuring in Nigeria*. Ibadan: Spectrum Books Limited and IFRA.

Osaghae, E. (1991). Ethnic Minorities and Federalism in Nigeria. *African Affairs, 90*, 237–258.

Osaghae, E. (1995). The Ogoni Uprising: Oil Politics, Minority Agitation and the Future of the Nigerian State. *African Affairs, 94*(376), 325–344.

Osaghae, E. (1998a). *Crippled Giant: Nigeria Since Independence*. London: Hurst Company.

Osaghae, E. (1998b). Managing Multiple Minority Problems in a Divided Society: The Nigerian Experience. *Journal of Modern African Studies, 36*(1), 1–24.

Osaghae, E. (2003). The State and Ethnic Autonomy in Nigeria. *Regional & Federal Studies, 13*(2), 84–105.

Osaghae, E. (2018, January). *Restructuring and True Federalism: Nigeria in Perspective*. Convocation Lecture at National Open University (NOUN), Abuja, Nigeria.

Osuntokun, J. (1979). The Historical Background of Nigerian Federalism. In A. Akinyemi, et al. (Eds.), *Readings on Federalism* (pp. 91–102). Lagos, Nigeria: The Nigerian Institute of International Affairs (NIIA).

Oyediran, O., & Olagunju, O. (1979). The Military and the Politics of Revenue Allocation. In O. Oyediran (Ed.), *Nigerian Government and Politics Under Military Rule, 1966–79*. London and Basingstoke: Macmillan.

Oyovbaire, S. (1983). Structural Change and Political Processes in Nigeria. *African Affairs, 82*(326), 3–28.

Oyovbaire, S. (1985). *Federalism in Nigeria: A Study in the Development of the Nigerian State*. London: Macmillan.

Panter-Brick, S. (1970). From Military Coup to Civil War, January 1966 to May 1967. In S. K. Panter-Brick (Ed.), *Nigerian Politics and Military Rule: Prelude to the Civil War*. London: The Athlone Press.

Phillips, A. (1971). Nigeria's Federal Fiscal Experience. *The Journal of Modern African Studies, 9*(3), 398–408.

Phillips, A. (1991). Managing Fiscal Federalism: Revenue Allocation Issues. *Publius: The Journal of Federalism, 21*, 103–111.

Post, K., & Vickers, M. (1973). *Structure and Conflict in Nigeria 1960–1965*. London: Heinemann.

Report of the Constitutional Conference. (2014). Published by *Premium Times* (Online).

Riker, W. (1964). *Federalism: Origin, Operation, Significance*. Boston: Little, Brown.

Rodney, W. (1972). *How Europe Underdeveloped Africa*. London: Bogle-L'Ouverture Publications.

Ross, M. (1999, January). The Political Economy of the Resource Curse. *World Politics, 51*, 279–322.

Ross, M. (2001, April). Does Oil Hinder Democracy? *World Politics, 53*, 325–361.

Sawer, G. (1969). *Modern Federalism*. London: C.A. Watts & Co.

Shakir, F. (2017). *The Iraqi Federation: Origin, Operation and Significance*. London and New York: Routledge.

Smith, B. (2004, April). Oil Wealth and Regime Survival in the Developing World, 1960–1999. *American Journal of Political Science, 48*(2), 232–246.

Stein, M. (1968). Federal Political Systems and Federal Societies. *World Politics, 20*(4), 721–747.

Stepan, A. (1999). Federalism and Democracy: Beyond the US Model. *Journal of Democracy, 10*(4), 19–34.

Stepan, A. (2001). *Arguing Comparative Politics*. Oxford: Oxford University Press.

Suberu, R. (1998). States' Creation and the Political Economy of Nigerian Federalism In K. Amuwo, et al. (Eds.), *Federalism and Political Restructuring in Nigeria*. Ibadan: Spectrum.

Suberu, R. (2001). *Federalism and Ethnic Conflict in Nigeria*. Washington, DC: United States Institute of Peace Press.

Suberu, R. (2004). Nigeria: Dilemmas of Federalism. In U. M. Amoretti & N. Bermeo (Eds.), *Federalism and Territorial Cleavages*. Baltimore and London: Johns Hopkins University Press.

Suberu, R. (2008). The Supreme Court and Federalism in Nigeria. *Journal of Modern African Studies, 46*(3), 451–485.

Turner, T. (1978). Commercial Capitalism and the 1975 Coup. In S. K. Panter-Brick (Ed.), *Soldiers and Oil: The Political Transformation of Nigeria*. London: Frank Cass.

Turner, T. (1980). Nigeria: Imperialism, Oil Technology and the Comprador State. In P. Nore & T. Turner (Eds.), *Oil and Class Struggle*. London: Zed Press.

Ukiwo, U. (2011). The Nigerian State, Oil and the Niger Delta Crisis. In C. Obi & S. Rustad (Eds.), *Oil and Insurgency in the Niger Delta*. London and New York: Zed Books.

UNGA 61/295. (2008). *United Nations Declaration on the Rights of Indigenous Peoples.*

United Nations Development Programme (UNDP). (2006). *Niger Delta Human Development Report.* Abuja: United Nations Development Programme.

Vanguard. (2014, August 21). Confab: We Have Shamed Our Critics—Jonathan. https://www.vanguardngr.com/2014/08/confab-shamed-critics-jonathan. Accessed on January 15, 2017.

Verney, D. (1995). Federalism, Federative Systems, and Federations: The United States, Canada, and India. *Publius: The Journal of Federalism, 25*(2), 81–97.

Vile, M. J. C. (1961). *The structure of American Federalism.* Oxford: Oxford University Press.

Warisu, A. (2016). Federal-State Relations in Nigerian Federalism. In O. Ibeanu & M. J. Kuna (Eds.), *Nigerian Federalism: Continuing Quest for Stability and Nation-Building*. Ibadan: Safari Books.

Watts, R. (1966). *New Federations: Experiments in the Commonwealth.* Oxford: Clarendon Press.

Watts, R. (1998). Federalism, Federal Systems and Federations. *Annual Review of Political Science, 1*(117–37), 121.

Watts, R. (1999). *Comparing Federal Systems*, 2nd ed. Montreal and Kingston: McGill-Queen's University Press.

Watts, R. (2003). Introduction: Comparative Research and Fiscal Federalism. *Regional and Federal Studies, 13*(4), 1–6.

Welch, C. (1995). The Ogoni and Self-Determination: Increasing Violence in Nigeria. *Journal of Modern African Studies, 33*(4), 635–649.

Wheare, K. (1962). Federalism and the Making of Nations. In A. W. Macmahon (Ed.), *Federalism: Mature and Emergent.* New York: Russell & Russell.

Wheare, K. (1963). *Federal Government* (4th ed.). London: Oxford University Press.

Wheare, K. (1968). *Legislatures.* London: Oxford University Press.

White, G., & Taylor, S. (2001). Well-Oiled Regimes: Oil & Uncertain Transitions in Algeria & Nigeria. *Review of African Political Economy, 28*(89), 323–344.

Williams, G. (1976). Nigeria: A Political Economy. In G. Williams (Ed.), *Nigeria: Economy and Society*. London: Rex Collings.

Woelk, J. (2004). Federalism and Consociationalism as Tools for State Reconstruction? The Case of Bosnia and Herzegovina. In G. Alan Tarr, R. F. Williams, & J. Marka (Eds.), *Federalism, Subnational Constitutions, and Minority Rights*. Westport, CT, and London: Praeger.

Yates, D. (1996). *The Rentier State in Africa: Oil Rent Dependency and Neocolonialism in the Republic of Gabon*. Trenton: Africa World Press.

Yoruba Assembly, Afenifere Renewal Group and Yoruba Academy. (2014). *Regional Autonomy or Nothing*. https://www.premiumtimesng.com/docs_download/Regional%20Autonomy%20or%20Nothing%20final%20PDF.Pdf. Accessed on April 20, 2015.

Index

D. Babalola, *The Political Economy of Federalism in Nigeria*, Federalism and Internal Conflicts, https://doi.org/10.1007/978-3-030-05493-9

The manufacturer's authorised representative in the EU is Springer
Nature Customer Service Centre GmbH, Europaplatz 3, 69115 Heidelberg,
Germany. If you have any concerns regarding our products, please
contact ProductSafety@springernature.com

Printed and bound by CPI Group (UK) Ltd, Croydon, CR0 4YY
30/09/2026
02225442-0001